Hands-On Windows Programming Series (HOWPS):

Book 1:
Introduction to
Window
Programming

For Users of Microsoft® Visual C++™ Development System for Windows™

Richard P. Braden

Wordware Publishing, Inc.

Library of Congress Cataloging-in-Publication Data

Braden, Richard P.
   Introduction to Window programming / by Richard P. Braden.
       p.   cm. -- (Hands-on Windows programming series ; book 1)
   Includes index.
   ISBN 1-55622-432-X
   1. Windows (Computer programs).   2. Microsoft Windows
   (Computer file).   I. Title.   II. Series.
   QA76.76.W56B72   1994
   005.265--dc20
                                94-17674
                                  CIP

ISBN 1-55622-432-X

10 9 8 7 6 5 4 3 2 1

9410

Permission has been requested and received from the Microsoft Corporation, Redmond, Washington, to
include a description and portions of the software found in the Visual C++ DSFW, program
SAMPLES\PRNTFILE, procedures GetPrinterDC( ), AbortProc( ), and AbortDlg( ).
MS, MS-DOS, and the Windows logo are registered trademarks and Windows and Visual C++ are
trademarks of the Microsoft Corporation, Redmond, Washington.
Other product names mentioned are used for identification purposes only and may be trademarks of their
respective companies.

All inquiries for volume purchases of this book should be addressed to Wordware
Publishing, Inc., at 1506 Capital Avenue, Plano, Texas 75074. Telephone inquiries
may be made by calling:

(214) 423-0090

TABLE OF CONTENTS

The programming information in this book is based on information for developing applications for Windows 95 made public by Microsoft as of May 1994. Since this information was made public before the final release of the product, there may have been changes to some of the programming interfaces by the time the product is finally released. We encourage you to check the updated development information that should be part of your development system for resolving issues that might arise.

The end-user information in this book is based on information on Windows 95 made public by Microsoft as of May 1994. Since this information was made public before the release of the product, we encourage you to visit your local bookstore at that time for updated books on Windows 95.

If you have a modem or access to the Internet, you can always get up-to-the-minute information on Windows 95 direct from Microsoft on WinNews:

On Compuserve:	GO WINNEWS
On the Internet:	ftp://ftp.microsoft.com/PerOpSys/Win_News/Chicago
	bttp://www.microsoft.com
On AOL:	keyword WINNEWS
On Prodigy:	jumpword WINNEWS
On Genie:	WINNEWS file area on Windows RTC

You can also subscribe to Microsoft's WinNews electronic newsletter by sending Internet email to news@microsoft.nwnet.com and putting the words SUBSCRIBE WINNEWS in the text of the email.

Foreword

In January 1993 we began to assemble the data, programs, and text for this series about MS Windows application programming using the Visual C++ Development System for Windows (DSFW). At that time Windows 3.1 was coming into vogue, and the principal compiler was Visual C++ Version 1.0, an offshoot of the old Software Development Kit (SDK).

Today Windows 95 (Chicago Windows) is in distribution and the Visual C++ DSFW Version 1.5 enjoys wide usage. We are pleased that all the programs that were written for this series compiled and executed using both DSFW versions and both Windows versions. There are two reasons for this success:

- This series teaches windows basics, and the basics remain unchanged from application upgrade to upgrade.
- The Microsoft Corporation has kept its pledge for total backward compatibility and systemwide interoperability.

We appreciate that.

This series is written for Visual C++ DSFW developers.

Book 1 Abbreviations

DSFW	Development System for Windows
HOWPS	Hands-On Window Programming Series
MB	Megabyte
MDI	Multiple Document Interface
MFC	Microsoft Foundation Classes
MSVC	Microsoft Visual C
PPE	Professional Programmer's Edition
SE	Standard Edition
VWB	Visual Workbench

Book 1: Introduction to Window Programming

- **Program Sequences**
- **Main Windows**
- **Popup Dialog and Message Boxes**
- **Printing Hardcopy**
- **Advantages of STRICT typecasting**
- **SETUP1 Installation Program Sample**

Using:

- **MS Visual C++ Workbench (VWB)**
- **AppStudio (Dialog Editor)**
- **Integrated Debugger**

This series addresses applications development subjects which are common to three Microsoft Corporation Compiler/Linker releases:

- **Visual C++ Version 1.0 Standard Edition**, which features an upgraded Fast Compiler.

- **Visual C++ Version 1.0 Professional Programmer's Edition**, which includes both the Fast Compiler and standard MS Optimizing Compiler, plus an assortment of new software tools that are accessed within the Visual C++ Workbench.

- **Visual C++ Version 1.5 Professional Edition**, which is an upgrade to the Version 1.0 Professional Programmer's Edition. This upgrade supports 16-bit applications development on PCs equipped with:

  - The MS-DOS operating system with Windows 3.1, or
  - Windows 95 (Chicago) with its own built-in operating system, or
  - Windows NT.

All versions use the same Visual C++ Workbench.

Section 1

Introduction

ABOUT THIS SERIES   This series presents the most common window programming topics in the following books:

- Introduction to Window Programming
- Child Windows
- Painting the Screen
- Transferring Data To and From Windows
- Mouse, Timer, and Keyboard Inputs
- Text and Special Fonts, Menus, Printing
- AppStudio Graphics Editor Tutorial
- Multiple Document Interface (MDI)
- Large Project Architecture and Special Topics
- Master Index/Cross-reference Guide to Books 1-9

ABOUT BOOK 1

This book resolves many of the developer's unanswered questions about window programming and relieves some of the discomfort encountered as one embarks on a window programming career. Windows requires that the developer leave the relative comfort of the known and venture into the unknown.

Learning from the MS Visual C++ DSFW, Versions 1.0 or 1.5, is like trying to drink from a fire hose. There is so much to learn; it is an unforgettable experience. This book provides the developer with step-by-step directions to produce an initial, successful window programming experience. This is only the first of a series of Visual C++ DSFW programming books—it addresses the narrow issues of main windows, popup dialog boxes, and popup message boxes. It demonstrates dialog box creation with the Dialog Editor, printing of

1

a file using MS-DOS procedures, codeview debugging, STRICT compilation/ linking, and how installation SETUP programs are created.

This book begins with a short description of the "Main Window" variations that a developer may select as the entry point for a windows application. A brief project named MAINMAIN is provided so the developer may experiment with the main window.

Next, this book describes an in-line program named PAYUP that computes the time it will take to pay off a simple interest loan. It was originally written as a non-windowed application. This is a no-frills program, but the windowed version makes excellent use of popup dialog and message boxes. It also teaches a great deal about program sequencing within a windows application.

Project PAYUP prompts the user for three inputs:

- Amount of the loan
- Yearly interest rate
- Proposed monthly payment (PI—principal and interest)

Then PAYUP computes and displays to the user the number of months required to pay off the loan. The user has the option to rerun the program using all new inputs or adjusting only the proposed monthly payment. When all reruns are complete, the user may request a printed copy of the loan amortization table. This project demonstrates how to print a file using MS-DOS procedures. In another book in this series printing with the modern Microsoft Foundation Class software is presented, since the developer will eventually make the transition to the newer prepackaged foundation class software for new printing applications.

Next, this book describes in projects MAN-EDIT, AUTOEDIT, and NEWEDIT how the developer may create dialog boxes manually, edit manually-created dialog boxes in the automated AppStudio Dialog Editor, or create totally new dialog boxes in the Dialog Editor.

Next, in project DEBUG, the integrated Codeview Debugger is presented. This debugger works totally within the VWB and represents a quantum leap in the use of source code debuggers.

A STRICT typecasting example is shown to encourage developers to use STRICT as a standard programming pragma.

Finally, the code used to prepare SETUP1 for this book is included to show a typical setup or installation program. SETUP1 uses the old MS-DOS macros to copy files; the new "LZEXPAND" file manipulation series is explained in a later book.

REFERENCE BOOKS   The HOWPS frequently references two books that are the foundation of window programming. The developer is expected to consult these books to fully understand the procedures being exercised. It is our understanding that these texts will not be reissued for Windows 4.0, so the 3.1 versions are the latest:

- *Programming Windows 3.1*, Third Edition, Charles Petzold, Microsoft Corporation, Microsoft Press (983 pages). This book will be referred to in this series as "Petzold 3.1."

- *Developing Windows 3.1 Applications with Microsoft C/C++*, Second Edition, Brent Rector (Wise-Owl Consulting), Sams Publishing (1330 pages). This book will be referred to as "Rector 3.1."

Although these texts were written before the introduction of the complete Visual C++ DSFW, everything in them is up-to-date in terms of source-coding techniques for Windows 3.1, Windows 95, and Windows NT.

The earlier Windows 3.0 versions of these texts are out-of-date; use the 3.1 versions exclusively.

TEXT DIFFICULTY LEVEL

EXPECTED DEVELOPER CAPABILITIES   This book assumes that the developer knows a great deal about C programming. The developer must also know how to operate MS Windows because the Visual C++ DSFW is embedded in windows, normally in first-tier directory MSVC.

The developer need not be knowledgeable about the applications listed below, but initial familiarity aids the learning process. This book leads the developer through samples that use these tools and recommends further reading:

- Visual C++ Workbench (VWB)
- Integrated Visual C++ Debugger within the VWB
- Dialog Editor (a part of the AppStudio)

COMPUTER MACHINERY CAPABILITIES   The machine hosting the Visual C++ DSFW must be a 386 or 486 PC and have sufficient hard disk space (up to 48 MB if Version 1.0 is loaded completely on the hard disk, and up to 120 MB if Version 1.5 is completely on the hard disk). If the PC is equipped with a CD-ROM reader only 5 MB may be required on the hard disk to support Visual C++.

The handwriting is on the wall! You will not be able to operate any heavy-duty compiler/linker sold by an American software manufacturer in the future without a CD-ROM player. You may get by for now by copying large amounts of software from a series of installation disks, but this will limit the space available on the hard disk for your other applications. We suggest that you install a CD-ROM reader in your PC.

TIP: If you are using MS-DOS and Windows 3.1 to host the DSFW, then 4 megabytes of RAM on your PC is sufficient. If you upgrade to Windows 95 to host the DSFW then 8 megabytes of RAM is a necessity — 4 megabytes runs too slowly.

VISUAL C++ VERSION 1.0 STANDARD EDITION (SE) and PROFESSIONAL PROGRAMMER'S EDITION (PPE) The HOWPS addresses both editions. The principal differences between the two Visual C++ Version 1.0 editions are:

- **Compilers** The SE includes an upgraded Fast Compiler only, while the PPE has both the Fast and full Standard C Optimizing Compiler.

- **Tools** Both versions have the integrated tools which are accessed in the VWB (AppStudio, AppWizard, Integrated Debugger, etc.). The PPE also has additional tools (Heap Walker, Spy, Hotspot Editor, etc.) which may be useful later in one's career.

- **MS-DOS Compatibility** Only the PPE has the ability to create programs for non-windowed applications.

- **Debugging Capability** The PPE includes old codeview debuggers for debugging both windowed and non-windowed applications. Both are surpassed by the new integrated debugger in the VWB, and are of no immediate value to the developer.

VISUAL C++ VERSION 1.5 PROFESSIONAL EDITION The new professional edition uses the same VWB, AppStudio (Dialog Editor), and Codeview Debugger presentations as Version 1.0. There is greatly expanded tools capability that the developer may use in the future, but this will not be demonstrated during the HOWPS tutorials/demonstrations.

For purposes of this series, any of the three editions will suffice.

FURTHER REFERENCES   For about $60 additional, the four-volume set of Microsoft Visual C++ Programmer's Reference Manuals may be purchased through the Microsoft Press or at any good computer book store. All this information is included in the on-line help (which explains why the complete Visual C++ Version 1.0 package requires about 48 MB of disk space and the Version 1.5 package requires 110-120 MB). When a baffling programming problem occurs, the hardcopy reference manuals are irreplaceable. The four volumes are:

- Volume 1—Overview
- Volume 2—Functions
- Volume 3—Messages, Structures, and Macros
- Volume 4—Resources

Within the group of manuals that all purchasers receive with the MS Visual C++ DSFW is a manual entitled "User's Guides: Visual Workbench and AppStudio." This is an important manual because it introduces the developer to the enhanced text-editor, the Visual Workbench that the developer will use to create all applications.

TEXT SCOPE   The developer is introduced to the Visual Workbench (VWB) in which all types of windows programs are created. There is a discussion on how to bring old windows projects originally built with older C compilers into Visual C++ for updating and recompilation, and techniques for spawning new projects from old projects. For totally new projects the AppWizard is demonstrated, a tool that creates a complete set of windows development system boilerplate files. The fourth type of VWB project shown is the administrative type, the project that will be used only for text editing, etc., where no source code compilation/linking will ever occur. All of the source code listings shown in the HOWPS were annotated and printed from administrative type VWB projects.

Two primary tools that support the VWB are briefly described and exercised:

AppStudio   This tool is both a dialog editor and graphics editor. This book will describe how to prepare dialog boxes in the dialog editor; graphics editor instruction will follow in Book 7 in the series.

Integrated Visual C++ Debugger   Most developers resort to the source code debugger only after all other avenues of approach have failed and the program is performing incorrectly. The thrust of this introduction is to show that the Integrated Visual C++ Source Code Debugger is available within the VWB to single-step or giant-step through an ailing program. This tool is a quantum jump in on-line debugging capability.

The Integrated Visual C++ Debugger does not provide for the "two screen" presentation option that older codeview debuggers offered; however, the MS Windows "toggle" between the source code in the VWB and the display that the source code creates is always available by pressing **Alt+Tab**, the universal toggle between the current application and the last application.

This book does not address the Microsoft Foundation Class (MFC) Libraries until Book 6 since they are an advanced topic, nor does it dwell on C++ programming. Once the developer becomes addicted to Visual C, learning to program in C++ and building integrated programs using the MFCs is a natural progression in one's professional development.

Transferring HOWPS Book 1 Files to Your Hard Disk:

The enclosed diskette, SETUP1, copies files to these directories:

- To C:____\SOURCE, subdirectories NEW-PROJ and WINDLIST.
- To C:____\SOURCE\BOOK1, subdirectories MAINMAIN, PAYUPNW, PAYUP1, PAYUP2, PAYUP3, MAN-EDIT, AUTOEDIT, NEWEDIT, DEBUG, STRICT, and SETUP1.

  The first-tier directory shown as "____" above is usually named **MSVC**.

To perform the copy task in Windows 3.1:

1. Insert the enclosed diskette in a diskette drive (A: or B:).
2. Enter Windows and Program Manager.
3. Pick menu **File|Run**. The Run window appears.
4. Type in the Command Line **A:\SETUP1** or **B:\SETUP1**.
5. Pick pushbutton **OK** on the Run window.

   Enter the directory name "**C:\MSVC**," then pick **OK**. The setup program informs the user after each successful directory creation and after each successful copy of files to that directory.

To perform the copy task in Windows 95:

1. Insert the enclosed diskette in a diskette drive (A: or B:).
2. Enter Windows 95.
3. At the lower left, pick menu **Start|Run**. The Run window appears.
4. Type in the Command Line **A:\SETUP1** or **B:\SETUP1**.
5. Pick pushbutton **OK** on the Run window.

Enter the directory name "**C:\MSVC**," then pick **OK**.

Conventions Used in This Book:

The command for picking a menu at the top of the screen with the mouse cursor, then picking a particular vertical menu item (for example, menu "File" followed by menu item "Open"), will be written as "Pick **File|Open**."

Enabling/Disabling Source Code:

Throughout this series the developer is asked to "disable" source code. For example, to disable the statement DialogBox( ), the developer should place the universal remark characters before and after the statement:

```
/* Dialogbox( ) */
```

If the source code is initially disabled and the developer is asked to "enable" the code, the remark characters should be deleted.

Standard Prefixes for Windows Variables:

These are the naming conventions commonly used in windows development. The third item on the list, "ha," a handle name passed to a function as an argument, has been added by the writer to make the source of each handle name more distinctive in the HOWPS code. See also Rector 3.1, p. 37, and Petzold 3.1, pp. 27-28:

Handles:

Prefix	Data Type	Meaning
h	HANDLE	16-bit unsigned integer
gh	GLOBALHANDLE (HWND)	handle declared at top of *.c file
ha	HANDLEARGUMENT (HWND)	handle passed to a function as an argument
lh	LOCALHANDLE (HWND)	handle declared within a function

Other:

Prefix	Data Type	Meaning
f	BOOLEAN	TRUE, FALSE
b	BYTE	eight bits
ch	CHAR	ASCII character
dw	DWORD	32-bit unsigned integer
l	LONG	32-bit signed integer
lp	FAR*	32-bit far (long) pointer
n	short	16-bit signed integer (counter)
pt	POINT	X and Y coordinates
sz	CHAR array	null terminated character string
w	WORD	16-bit unsigned integer

IMPORTANT PROCEDURES AND DIRECTORIES LISTINGS

The three procedures listed below are used frequently to execute the projects in this book.

- **New Project Loading Sequence**—How to bring a complete, executable project that is provided by this text or an example from another source into the Visual Workbench (VWB) the first time.

- **Creating New Projects**—How to create a basic set of five empty files that the developer modifies to serve her/his purposes.

- **View Copy of File WINDOWS.H**—How to create an administrative project that uses the VWB as a text editor only.

NEW PROJECT LOADING SEQUENCE This loading sequence is necessary because each project must be loaded the first time into the VWB as a new project. During this process the VWB records the path to the project and creates a list of the project files so the project may be opened thereafter with **File|Open**. The first time any project is loaded into the VWB, perform these tasks within the VWB main window:

1. In the VWB, pick **Project|New**.

2. The New Project window appears.

3. Pick **Browse...**. The Browse window appears. In the Directories: listbox pick the project path, e.g., C:\MSVC\SOURCE\BOOK1\ MAINMAIN, (or whatever first-tier directory the developer chose during SETUP1 to replace "MSVC") by picking each element in the string in order.

4. The makefile name appears in the File Name: listbox, but it is "grayed" because the VWB cannot determine if it is the correct makefile. Double-click on the grayed makefile name, which causes an exit from the Browse window.

5. The New Project window reappears and the selected project with its full path is shown in the Project Name: editbox. Pick **OK** to exit this window.

6. A Microsoft Visual C++ window appears, explaining that the project makefile already exists. Do you wish to overwrite it? Pick **Yes**.

7. The EDIT - <ProjectName.Mak> window appears. Pull down the selections on the List Files of Type: listbox and pick **All Files [*.*]**.

8. In the File Name: listbox double-click on these three files to place them in the Files in Project list: ***.DEF**, ***.C**, and ***.RC**.

9. Pick pushbutton **Close** to exit the Project Edit window.

For a few seconds a Scan Dependencies window will appear, then disappear.

The project is now correctly "pathed" to the VWB, and the project files are properly listed. Next time the project is worked, open it with **File|Open** or the left-most icon on the VWB toolbar.

CREATING NEW PROJECTS Within the VWB an application named AppWizard exists that creates a new project with 18 files. AppWizard is geared for work in the Microsoft Foundation Classes (MFC) software development area, which is an advanced topic and will be discussed in the later books in the HOWPS.

However, a special pseudo-project builder has been provided that creates a series of five files which are the starting point for a new project. These files contain a generic project name "GENERATE." To create a new project:

In Windows 3.1:

1. Get out of the VWB (minimize it) and into the Windows Program Manager.

2. In Program Manager, pick **File|Run**. A Run Application window appears.

3. In the Command Line: editbox type

   C:___\SOURCE\NEW-PROJ\NEW-PROJ.EXE

   where the "____" is the first-tier directory name in which the Visual C++ Development System for Windows (DSFW) is located. The standard name for this directory is **MSVC**.

In Windows 95:

1. Get out of the VWB (minimize it), and into the main window.

2. Pick **Start|Run**. A Run Application window appears.

3. In the **Command Line:** editbox type

   C:___\SOURCE\NEW-PROJ\NEW-PROJ.EXE.

   NEW-PROJ asks for a name for the new project with its complete path, checks that the project does not already exist, then creates the project. For example, if the developer wishes to create a new project named GOODTIME and the Visual C++ DSFW is located in directory MSVC, then the editbox entry in the first window of NEW-PROJ would be:

   C:\MSVC\SOURCE\GOODTIME

Five files are created (where * = project name GOODTIME):

- *.DEF, the resource definition file
- *.H, the project header file
- *.RC, the resource script file
- *.C, the main source code file
- *.MAK, the skeletal makefile

The next operation the developer should perform is the New Project Loading Sequence listed above, since this is a new project. This is accomplished within the VWB.

At this time, for practice, we suggest that you create project GOODTIME and perform the New Project Loading Sequence. After the New Project Loading Sequence is complete, edit each of the four source files (*.DEF, *.H, *.RC,

*.C) to eliminate the reference to the generic project name "GENERATE." Edit the files as shown below. The line numbers refer to Figure 1-1.

In the VWB pick **File|Open**. Under List Files of Type: pick **All Files [*.*]**. Then pick **goodtime.def** to bring the first file into the editor.

- File *.DEF (lines 001-011):
  - **Line 001** Change GENERATE to GOODTIME.
  - Delete **line 002**.
  - **Line 003** Change GENERATE to GOODTIME.
  - **Line 004** Describe project GOODTIME.

  (Save and close GOODTIME.DEF, then open GOODTIME.H for editing).

- File *.H (lines 101-107):
  - **Line 101** Change GENERATE to GOODTIME.
  - Delete **line 102**.

  (Save and close GOODTIME.H, then open GOODTIME.RC for editing).

- File *.RC (lines 201-224):
  - **Line 201** Change GENERATE to GOODTIME.
  - Delete **line 202**.
  - **Line 204** Change generate to goodtime.
  - **Lines 205, 207, 208** Change Generate to GoodTime.
  - **Lines 213, 214** Change Generate to GoodTime.
  - **Line 216** Enter your name after the copyright logo, "\251."

  (Save and close GOODTIME.RC, then open GOODTIME.C for editing).

- File *.C (lines 301-722):
  - **Line 301** Change GENERATE to GOODTIME and enter your name.
  - Delete **line 302**.
  - **Line 305** Change generate to goodtime.
  - **Lines 327, 328** Change Generate to GoodTime.
  - **Line 342** Change Generate to GoodTime in **2** places.

  (Save and close GOODTIME.C.)

Figure 1-1, Goodtime

```
001: ; GENERATE.DEF module-definition file -- used by LINK.EXE
002: ; Enter the new project name on the line above, and fill in
     ; name and description below.
```

```
003: NAME    Generate  ; Application's module name
004: DESCRIPTION  'Describe the project here'
005: EXETYPE WINDOWS    ; Required for all Windows  applications
006: STUB   'WINSTUB.EXE'; Generates error message if application
                         ; is run without Windows
007: ;CODE can be moved in memory and discarded/reloaded
008: CODE  PRELOAD MOVEABLE DISCARDABLE
009: ;DATA must be MULTIPLE if program invoked more than once
010: DATA  PRELOAD MOVEABLE MULTIPLE
011: HEAPSIZE     1024
/******************************************************************/

101: /* GENERATE.H (header file) */
102: /* Enter the new project name on the line above */

103: /* Enable the line below if this file is used to create dialog boxes or
menus in the Visual C++ Dialog Editor */

105: #define IDM_ABOUT      10
106: #define IDM_STARTSWITCH 15
107: #define IDD_DIALOG51    51


/******************************************************************/

201: /* GENERATE.RC (resource script file) */

202: /* Enter new file name on the line above, & replace GENERATE
     in: the include statement below, in the menuitem, and in the
     AboutBox. Put your name in the AboutBox. */

203: #include <windows.h>
204: #include "generate.h"

205: GenerateMenu MENU
206:   {POPUP       "&Begin"
207:     {MENUITEM "&About Generate...",              IDM_ABOUT
208:     MENUITEM  "&Start Generate ",         IDM_STARTSWITCH
209:     }
210:   }

211: AboutBox DIALOG 22, 17, 110, 55
212: STYLE DS_MODALFRAME | WS_CAPTION
213: CAPTION "About Generate"
214:   {CTEXT "Generate Application"       -1, 0, 5, 110, 8
215:   CTEXT "Microsoft Windows 3.1 and 4.0" -1, 0, 15, 110, 8
216:   CTEXT "Copyright \251 _____, 1994" -1, 0, 25, 110, 8
```

```
217:    PUSHBUTTON "OK"                      IDOK, 39, 36,  32, 14
218:    }

219: IDD_DIALOG51 DIALOG 50, 20, 150,60
220: STYLE DS_MODALFRAME | WS_CAPTION
221: CAPTION "Dialog Box #1"
222:    {CTEXT "Start Here"  -1, 0,15,150,8
223:    PUSHBUTTON "OK"    IDOK, 59, 40, 32, 14
224:    }


/**************************************************************/

301: /*  GENERATE.C, _____ */

302: /* Enter  new  file  name  on  the  line above, and  replace
     GENERATE  in  the  include  statement  and  the main  window
     description below */

303: #define STRICT
304: #include <windows.h>
305: #include "generate.h"

306: long FAR PASCAL _export WndProc(HWND, UINT, WPARAM, LPARAM);
307: BOOL FAR PASCAL _export AboutProc(HWND, UINT,WPARAM,LPARAM);
308: BOOL FAR PASCAL _export DialogOne(HWND, UINT,WPARAM,LPARAM);
309: long FAR PASCAL _export FirstChild(HWND,UINT,WPARAM,LPARAM);
310: HANDLE hInst;
311: HWND   ghWnd; /* Main window */
312: HWND ghChild; /* Child window */

313: int PASCAL
     WinMain(HINSTANCE hInstance,HINSTANCE hPrevInstance,
     LPSTR lpCmdLine, int nCmdShow)
314:    {MSG msg;
315:    WNDCLASS wc;
316:    ATOM aWndClass;
317:    if(!hPrevInstance)
318:      {/* Main window */
319:      wc.style = NULL; /* Or CS_VREDRAW | CS_HREDRAW */
320:      wc.lpfnWndProc = WndProc;
321:      wc.cbClsExtra = 0;
322:      wc.cbWndExtra = 0;
323:      wc.hInstance = hInstance;
324:      wc.hIcon = LoadIcon(NULL, IDI_APPLICATION);
325:      wc.hCursor = LoadCursor(NULL, IDC_ARROW);
326:      wc.hbrBackground = GetStockObject(WHITE_BRUSH);
327:      wc.lpszMenuName = "GenerateMenu";
```

13

```
328:     wc.lpszClassName = "GenerateWClass";
329:     aWndClass = RegisterClass(&wc);
330:     if(!aWndClass) MessageBox(NULL,
331:        "Failure to register Main Window Class.",NULL, MB_OK);

332:     /* Register child window class */
333:     wc.lpfnWndProc = FirstChild;
334:     wc.hIcon = NULL;
335:     wc.lpszMenuName = NULL;
336:     wc.lpszClassName = "ChildOneWClass";
337:     aWndClass = RegisterClass(&wc);
338:     if(!aWndClass) MessageBox(NULL,
339:        "Failure to register Child Window Class.",NULL,MB_OK);
340:     }

341:   hInst = hInstance;
342:   ghWnd=CreateWindow("GenerateWClass","Generate Application",
          WS_OVERLAPPEDWINDOW,   CW_USEDEFAULT,   CW_USEDEFAULT,
          CW_USEDEFAULT, CW_USEDEFAULT, NULL,  NULL, hInst, NULL);
343:   /* Make window visible; update its client area */
344:   ShowWindow(ghWnd,nCmdShow);/* or ghWnd,SW_SHOWMAXIMIZED */
345:   UpdateWindow(ghWnd);

346:   while(GetMessage(&msg, NULL, NULL, NULL))
347:     {TranslateMessage(&msg);
348:     DispatchMessage(&msg);
349:     }
350:   return(msg.wParam);
351:   } /* End of WinMain( )  */

/***************************************************************/

401: long FAR PASCAL _export
     WndProc(HWND haWnd, UINT msg, WPARAM wParam, LPARAM lParam)
402:   {DLGPROC lpProcAbout;/* Pointer to "AboutProc" function */
403:   DLGPROC lpProcOne; /* Pointer to "DialogOne" function */
404:   HWND lhPushB;  /* Pushbutton control */

405:   switch(msg)
406:     {case WM_COMMAND:
407:       if(wParam == IDM_ABOUT)
408:         {lpProcAbout = (DLGPROC)MakeProcInstance((FARPROC)
              AboutProc, hInst);
409:         DialogBox(hInst, "AboutBox", haWnd, lpProcAbout);
410:         FreeProcInstance((FARPROC)lpProcAbout);
411:         break;
412:         }
```

```
413:       else if(wParam == IDM_STARTSWITCH)
414:         { /* This is the point the menu sends control to */
415:         /* Create a dialog box */
416:         lpProcOne = (DLGPROC)MakeProcInstance((FARPROC)
                DialogOne, hInst);
417:         DialogBox(hInst,MAKEINTRESOURCE(IDD_DIALOG51),haWnd,
                lpProcOne);
418:         FreeProcInstance((FARPROC)lpProcOne);
419:         /* Create a child window with pushbutton */
420:         ghChild=CreateWindow("ChildOneWClass",NULL,WS_CHILD|
                WS_BORDER | WS_VISIBLE, 50,20,300,120, haWnd,NULL,
                hInst, NULL);
421:         lhPushB = CreateWindow("Button",   "OK",  WS_CHILD |
                WS_VISIBLE | BS_PUSHBUTTON, 120,90,60, 20,ghChild,
                (HMENU)IDOK, hInst, NULL);
422:         break;
423:         }
424:       else
425:         return(DefWindowProc(haWnd, msg, wParam, lParam));

426:     case WM_DESTROY:
427:       PostQuitMessage(0);
428:       break;
429:     default:
430:       return(DefWindowProc(haWnd, msg, wParam, lParam));
431:     }
432:   return NULL;
433:   } /* End of WndProc( ) */

/***************************************************************/

501: BOOL FAR PASCAL _export
     AboutProc(HWND haDlg,UINT msg, WPARAM wParam, LPARAM lParam)
502:   {switch(msg)
503:     {case WM_INITDIALOG:
504:       return TRUE;
505:     case WM_COMMAND:
506:       if(wParam == IDOK || wParam == IDCANCEL)
507:         {EndDialog(haDlg, TRUE);
508:         return TRUE;
509:         }
510:       break;
511:     }
512:   return FALSE;
513:   } /* End of AboutProc( ) */

/***************************************************************/
```

15

```
601: BOOL FAR PASCAL _export
     DialogOne(HWND haDlg,UINT msg, WPARAM wParam, LPARAM lParam)
602:   {switch(msg)
603:     {case WM_INITDIALOG:
604:       return TRUE;
605:     case WM_COMMAND:
606:       if(wParam == IDOK)
607:         {EndDialog(haDlg, TRUE);
608:         return TRUE;
609:         }
610:       break;
611:     }
612:   return FALSE;
613:   } /* End of DialogOne( ) */

/***************************************************************/

701: long FAR PASCAL _export
     FirstChild(HWND haChild,UINT msg,WPARAM wParam,LPARAM lParam)
702:   {HDC        hdc;
703:   PAINTSTRUCT ps;

704:   switch(msg)
705:     {case WM_COMMAND:
706:       if(wParam == IDOK)
707:         {DestroyWindow(haChild);
708:         break;
709:         }
710:       else
711:         return(DefWindowProc(haChild, msg, wParam, lParam));

712:     case WM_PAINT:
713:       hdc = BeginPaint(haChild, &ps);
714:         SetTextAlign(hdc, TA_CENTER);
715:         TextOut(hdc, 150, 40, "First Child Window", 18);
716:       EndPaint(haChild, &ps);
717:       break;

718:     default:
719:       return(DefWindowProc(haChild, msg, wParam, lParam));
720:     }
721:   return NULL;
722:   } /* End of FirstChild( ) */

/***************************************************************/
```

Figure 1-1:   Program Goodtime

Build the project by picking **Project|Rebuild All GOODTIME.EXE**. Then execute the project to ensure that all changes have been made properly in the source code. The project is now ready for work.

VIEW COPY OF FILE "WINDOWS.H"   MS Windows provides a text editor named Notepad to view/edit ASCII files, but WINDOWS.H is too large to fit into the Notepad editor. Therefore, a pseudo-project has been provided so the developer can view the giant WINDOWS.H file within the VWB, using it primarily as a text editor. The file has been renamed WINDLIST.DOC to ensure that it does not interact with actual compilation/linking events.

WINDOWS.H defines most of the reserved words in MS Visual C++ DSFW; additional words are defined in WINDOWX.H. Once this project is loaded into the VWB any reserved word, term, or expression may be located in the WINDOWS.H file using the VWB text editor search function.

Load the WINDLIST project into the VWB according to the New Project Loading Sequence described previously.

Thereafter, to view WINDLIST.DOC:

1. Enter the VWB.

2. Pick **Project|Open**.

3. Pick **C:___\SOURCE\WINDLIST\WINDLIST.MAK**. This action loads the administrative project WINDLIST.

4. Pick **File|Open WINDLIST.DOC**. The file appears in the VWB window.

DIRECTORIES LISTING   Figure 1-2 shows the software projects that are demonstrated or used in this book:

- Create New Projects
- View Copy of "WINDOWS.H"
- Section 4: Main Window Variations (MAINMAIN)
- Section 5: Projects PAYUP
- Section 6: Dialog Editor (MAN-EDIT, AUTOEDIT, NEWEDIT)
- Section 7: Integrated Debugger (DEBUG)
- Section 8: STRICT Typecasting (STRICT)

Create New Projects

In Windows, Program Manager:
Run: **C:____\SOURCE\NEW-PROJ\NEW-PROJ.EXE**

View Copy of "WINDOWS.H"

In Visual Workbench (VWB): Pick **Project|Open**
C:____\SOURCE\WINDLIST\WINDLIST.MAK
Pick **File|Open** WINDLIST.DOC

Section 4: Main Window Variations

In Visual Workbench (VWB): Pick **Project|Open**
C:____\SOURCE\BOOK1\MAINMAIN\MAINMAIN.MAK

Section 5: Projects PAYUP

In Visual Workbench (VWB): Pick **Project|Open**

C:____\SOURCE\BOOK1\PAYUP1\PAYUP1.MAK
C:____\SOURCE\BOOK1\PAYUP2\PAYUP2.MAK
C:____\SOURCE\BOOK1\PAYUP3\PAYUP3.MAK

Section 6: Dialog Editor

In Visual Workbench (VWB): Pick **Project|Open**

C:____\SOURCE\BOOK1\MAN-EDIT\MAN-EDIT.MAK
C:____\SOURCE\BOOK1\AUTOEDIT\AUTOEDIT.MAK
C:____\SOURCE\BOOK1\NEWEDIT\NEWEDIT.MAK

Section 7: Integrated Debugger

In Visual Workbench (VWB): Pick **Project|Open**
C:____\SOURCE\BOOK1\DEBUG\DEBUG.MAK

Section 8: STRICT Typecasting

In Visual Workbench (VWB): Pick **Project|Open**
C:____\SOURCE\BOOK1\STRICT\STRICT.MAK

Figure 1-2: Book 1 projects

Section 2

Getting Started

PC CONFIGURATION FOR SOFTWARE DEVELOPMENT

This section outlines the important software configuration considerations for MS Windows and the Visual C++ DSFW.

Configuring MS Windows   The MS Windows default installation (3.1 or Windows 95) is satisfactory for all windows software development so long as the installer selects the proper screen driver.

The proper screen driver is "Standard VGA," which produces a screen 640 pixels wide by 480 pixels high. No matter how high the definition capability of the monitor, the most-coarse setting (Standard VGA) must be selected when programming for windows, for this reason: All current window applications are written to fit on the screen with the smallest number of pixels (640 x 480). When a person who uses the software application selects the Super VGA drive for his/her monitor, the application's windows occupy the same number of pixels; consequently those windows developed on a VGA screen appear smaller on the Super VGA screen and progressively smaller on the higher-definition screens.

This is an acceptable aberration to the user. But if the original software developer sets his/her screen to Super VGA or a higher definition and develops all windows based on that higher definition, window sizes are embedded into the program that may overrun the screen of a machine whose display is set to "Standard VGA." This is quite inconvenient for the Standard VGA user. There are techniques for measuring the screen definition and resetting the application's window pixel dimensions to produce a consistent window size (for some, but not all classes of windows), but that level of programming will be achieved by most readers at a later time. For now, the reader should set her/his display to Standard VGA.

To determine which display driver is in use on a PC:

In Windows 3.1:

1. Enter Windows.
2. Pick the **Accessories Group**.
3. Pick the **Windows Setup** icon.
4. Read the entry after **Display:**. If it is "VGA," the PC is set to Standard VGA. If not VGA, then pick **Options**, which produces a list of screen drivers. Pick the **VGA driver** from the list. If the VGA driver is not present on your machine, Windows will ask you to load Diskette #1 from the Windows 3.1 installation package so the VGA driver may be loaded. Escape with **OK**s.

In Windows 95:

There is a Windows Setup icon present after picking **Start|Programs| Acces|Windows Setup**, but this does not produce a window capable of resetting the screen resolution to 640 x 480. Consult the Windows 95 documentation on this item.

TIP: Some modern PC hardware manufacturers, such as Gateway, have included a software program named "Set Res" with their computer deliveries. Set Res addresses the graphics card provided by the manufacturer directly and allows immediate transfer from VGA to any other monitor resolution supported by the monitor + graphics card. This is a necessary enhancement because many software developers choose VGA while performing development tasks and switch to a much higher resolution for other applications.

Configuring the MS Visual C++ DSFW   Version 1.0 was offered by the manufacturer on 14 or 20 diskettes for transfer to a hard disk, or on one CD-ROM. If the developer purchased the CD-ROM packaging of Version 1.0, the SETUP provided a "minimum installation" where only 5 MB of data is transferred to the hard disk and an additional 40+ MBs are accessed directly from the CD-ROM reader. However, the buyer also has the option of transferring all the system to the hard disk and operating from there.

With the advent of version 1.5, the only package offered is one CD-ROM (no diskettes), since over 100 MB of data is included. Again, the buyer is offered the opportunity to transfer all 100+ MBs to the hard disk during installation, but this is an unlikely choice. The "minimum installation" is the reasonable choice for version 1.5, where 5 MB of data is transferred to the hard disk and the remainder is accessed from the CD-ROM reader. The 5 MB includes the VWB plus the hooks to retrieve all the necessary compilers, tools, and helps from the CD-ROM.

There are some slight differences between versions 1.0 and 1.5. For example, version 1.0 eliminated the need for the WX Server, which is normally placed in the Windows Startup group and incorporated it internally into the DSFW. Version 1.5 placed the WX Server back into service and put it in the Windows Startup group again.

Version 1.5 is installed as a stand-alone application; it uses nothing from previous versions. It also removes the clutter of old, unused files from the hard disk so no unnecessary files remain from the previous DSFW installation.

Speed of compiler/linker operation is *not* an issue in this hard disk installation versus CD-ROM installation discussion. No development time is saved by placing the entire DSFW on a hard disk versus reading from the CD-ROM on demand.

After-Loading Checks (Windows 3.1 with Visual C++ DSFW)

AUTOEXEC.BAT After the DSFW is loaded, check the autoexec.bat file for the presence of a TMP subdirectory "set" statement.

1. Pick the Notepad icon, then click **File|Open** in the Notepad window.

2. In the File Name: edit box, type: **C:\AUTOEXEC.BAT**. Pick the **OK** pushbutton to load the file into Notepad. Check for the presence of this statement:

   ```
   SET TMP=C:\MSVC\TMP
   ```

3. Save the new AUTOEXEC.BAT file by picking **File|Save** in the Notepad window. Close Notepad by picking **File|Exit**.

SYSTEM.INI Reopen Notepad, and open file C:\WINDOWS\ SYSTEM.INI. Move to the section marked [386Enh] or [486Enh], etc. Make sure these two statements appear in the file:

```
DEVICE=C:\MSVC\BIN\DOSXNT.386 (or 486, etc.)
DEVICE=C:\MSVC\BIN\MMD.386 (or 486, etc.)
```

Providing a Swapping Directory In addition to placing the "SET TMP =C:\MSVC\TMP" statement in AUTOEXEC.BAT, the developer must check for the presence of subdirectory C:\MSVC\TMP on the hard disk. If it does not exist, the reader must create it to provide a scratch file location (swapping directory) for the VWB. Without this directory the VWB will not work properly.

After-Loading Checks (Windows 95 with Visual C++ DSFW)

There appear to be no after-loading checks when the DSFW is loaded on Windows 95.

Windows 3.1—Redistributing Icons If the developer loads all seven or eight options listed in the version 1.0 Visual C++ Installation Options list, the Microsoft Visual C++ group which is formed at the end of the installation has up to 21 icons in it. With version 1.5 the number of icons increases to about 90. Since the developer will probably operate from the VWB exclusively, only *one* of the icons is used at this time, the icon marked Visual C++, which is the entry point for the Visual Workbench.

The writer recommends this Windows Program Manager display option: Open the group named "Main" that was originally created with the new MS Windows 3.1 installation and empty it of most of its original icons (place them into the Accessories group by dragging them from Main to Accessories). Place into the Main group only this select group of icons (for example):

- File Manager
- DOS Prompt
- Notepad (to view/edit system files)
- A spreadsheet
- A database
- A word processor
- Visual C++ icon
- Communications icons (modem, FAX, etc.)
- Icons from any other major software applications on your PC.

Leave the Main group open on the Program Manager window at all times.

This arrangement is shown on Figure 2-1, after version 1.5 was loaded with its 90 icons. The icons appear in five groups across the lower portion of the Program Manager screen.

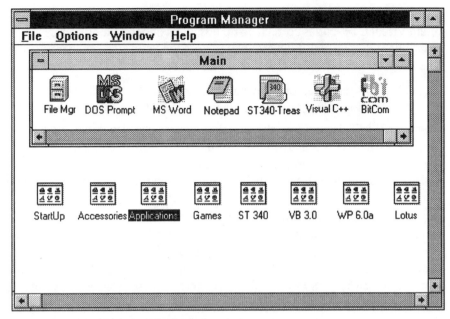

Figure 2-1 Sample Program Manager window setup

TIP: Any time the Program Manager or lower-level windows are rearranged or resized, there is a short sequence the developer should execute to save the settings:

1. In Program Manager pick **Options|Save Settings on Exit**. A check mark will appear to the left of the words "Save Settings on Exit" because this is a toggle.

2. In Program Manager system menu, pick **-|Close**.

3. The Exit Windows window appears. Click on **Cancel**. Do *not* click on **OK**.

4. Windows returns to the Program Manager window. Click on **Options|Save Settings on Exit** again, and the check mark to the left of "Save Settings..." disappears. The toggle is now turned off.

5. The new window arrangement is saved. Continue with work in windows.

IMPORTANT STEP: The developer must check that the working directory of the Visual C++ icon is correct. To do this, click once on the Visual C++ icon to highlight it, then pick **File|Properties** from the Program Manager window. The Program Item Properties window will appear.

The Working Directory *may* incorrectly read: "C:\MSVC\BIN"
The Working Directory should read: "C:\MSVC\SOURCE"

where "MSVC" represents the directory where the developer loaded the Visual C++ DSFW originally. If the settings are incorrect, edit them. Pick **OK** to close the Program Item Properties window. The VWB now has the proper path to the source code, which will be retained in subdirectory SOURCE. Some of the other 21 or 90 icons included with Visual C++ DSFW may also have improper working directories in their Program Item Properties listings. For example, some will show a working directory of MSVC\BIN, which leads nowhere. Do not be concerned with this unless a particular icon fails to produce the desired result when it is executed, since most of the icons never use the working directory path information. Very few of these icons are used by the developer during the life of the DSFW.

Windows 95—Redistributing Icons Consult the Windows 95 documentation to redistribute icons.

Disabling VWB Tabs If the developer dislikes Tabs in the VWB, they may be disabled and replaced with blank spaces within *all* project sets by doing the following:

1. Enter the VWB.

2. Pick **Options|Editor**. *Do not pick Project and open a project!*

3. Pick **Insert Spaces**, which deselects the default **Keep Tabs**.

4. Pick **OK** to exit the Editor window.

5. Close the VWB.

This disables all Tabs in future imported or newly created source code in all projects.

To disable the Tabs in one particular project:

1. Enter the VWB.

2. Pick **Project|Open** and open a project.

3. Pick **Options|Editor**.

4. Pick **Insert Spaces**.

5. Pick **OK** to exit the Editor window.

6. Resume work on the project.

Disabling the Browser Database   If the developer decides to disable this tool (it consumes time at every recompilation of a project):

1. Enter the VWB.

2. Pick **Options|Project**.

3. Pick **Compiler**. The Compiler Options window appears.

4. Under **Category:** pick **Listing Files**.

5. Deselect **Browser Information** by picking its checkbox.

6. Pick **OK** at top right of Compiler Options window to exit.

7. Pick **OK** at top right of Project Options window to exit.

Checking the Windows Startup Group   Visual C++ DSFW version 1.0 deleted the requirement for "WX Server" in the Windows Startup group by including it internally, but Version 1.5 elected to restore it and place it in the Startup group. This macro enables execution of a program within the VWB. If programs cannot be executed from within a project, check for the existence of WX Server in the Startup group.

VISUAL WORKBENCH (VWB)

Many of the important software tools and helps developed over the years by Microsoft are now accessible within pull-down menus or "buttons" in the VWB. For example, no longer is it necessary for the developer to exit the editor to peruse the on-line "helps." The real power behind MS Windows development concepts emerges with the ability of the VWB to access multiple tools/editors/helps and integrate the project within one central VWB main window.

Open the VWB now by picking the Visual C++ icon. As soon as the window is opened, pick the up-arrow at the top-right corner to maximize the window. Always maximize the VWB main window.

The VWB is the same for all versions of the Visual C++ DSFW. These VWB items are discussed below:

- Menu Bar, which is the group of 10 menus directly below the VWB window caption (title bar)
- Toolbar, immediately below the Menu Bar
- Entering the VWB for the first time
- Creating various types of projects within the VWB:
  - Importing project files built originally with older compilers, such as the MS C/C++ 7.0 Compiler and 3.1 Software Development Kit, and transferred to the VWB
  - New projects initiated within the VWB using application AppWizard. This is shown for information only; use the **CREATING NEW PROJECTS** procedure, **NEW-PROJ** at the front of this book, rather than AppWizard at this time (AppWizard creates 18 files—New-Proj creates 5).
  - Creating "successive" projects, where project "B" is a clone of project "A," with small modifications
  - Creating administrative type projects (ones that will never be used for compiling and linking source code)
- Preparation for integrated debugging

VWB Menu Bar   There are 10 pull-down menus shown across the top of the VWB. They are explained in detail in the User's Guides, VWB, pp. 59-198:

- The File and Edit menus work exactly like those in any word processor. Edit is applied only to a file. When one "edits" the project architecture, that editing is accomplished under the Project menu.
- The View menu controls the VWB display. The Toolbar (across the top of the VWB) and the Status Bar (across the bottom of the VWB) may be hidden or displayed, based on the toggle settings in **View**. Both should be displayed normally (not hidden).
- The Project menu is the first place the developer goes to start work in the VWB, and the next-to-the-last place visited when the work is complete; all project compilation, linking, and execution occurs there. The last pick before exiting the VWB is **File|Exit**.
- The Browse menu only has significance with large programs. It aids the developer in finding specific entries in the project file set. The text find/search capability on the Toolbar deals with one file at a time; the text search capability in **Browse** searches all project files.

- The integrated Debug menu is of interest after a project has been successfully cleared of syntax problems and debugging is required to expose logic/sequential errors. The debugger is discussed in Section 7.
- The Tools menu is the entry point into the "AppStudio," the tool for editing both dialog boxes and graphics presentations. Dialog box editing will be discussed in Section 6 in this book; graphics editing is the subject of a later book.
- The Options menu has some important settings under menu item **Project**. They include:
  - Ensuring that the Build Mode is set to "Debug" so the integrated debugger may be used if necessary. Only when a project is ready for release should the Build Mode be reset to "Release." This eliminates large quantities of embedded debugging code from the final product.
  - The Project Type should always be "Windows application [.EXE]."
  - The Memory Model is already set to "Medium" and should only be changed for very large, single-segment projects.
  - The default compiler is the Fast Compiler, and it may be necessary to convert to the Optimizing Compiler if the project being created becomes large. The Fast Compiler appears to have some subtle nuisances that the Optimizing Compiler cures when compiling larger projects. To convert to the Optimizing Compiler:
    - Under **Options**, pick **Project**. The Project Options window appears.
    - Pick pushbutton **Compiler**. The Compiler Options window appears.
    - At the lower right the words **Code Generator:** are shown. The default setting is Auto Select*, which means that the Fast Compiler is normally invoked.
    - Pick the arrow at the right end of the box. Four options are now shown. Pick the option **Optimizing Compiler**.
    - Exit by picking **OK** in the Compiler Options window and the Project Options window.

TIP: The Optimizing Compiler takes a few seconds more to compile but it seems to have all the bugs worked out. The Fast Compiler is there to outperform competitors for benchmark testing. The Optimizing Compiler is recommended for all Visual C++ compiling.

- The Options|Directories menu/menu item will never change during the development, but it must be correct the first time for all elements of the build to handshake properly. All elements in this editbox are copied from file C:\WINDOWS\MSVC.INI.

- The Window menu is of interest only when the integrated debugger is in action. This will be discussed in Section 7 in this book.

- The Help menu assists the developer in eight different areas, but these are subdivided into five relatively insignificant "helps" and three big "helps." In each case the Search menu item is the key to finding information quickly. The big helps are:

  - **Windows 3.1 SDK**   This is C language help, the contents of Volume 2 of the Programmer's Reference.

  - **C/C++ Language**   This is Volume 3 of the Programmer's Reference.

  - **Foundation Classes**   This is information related to the Microsoft Foundation Classes (MFCs).

VWB Toolbar   The Toolbar is described in the VWB User's Guide, pages 60-63. It includes 13 icons and one edit box which are clustered into four groups:

- The first three on the left perform file operations. Each duplicates a function included in the File menu:
  - Project files display (*.DEF, *.RC, *.C)
  - Open file
  - Save file

- The editbox/pulldown scroll with the one "binocular" icon is the Find/Search mechanism. This function is not duplicated elsewhere.

- The next three perform the most common project functions, all of which are duplicated in the Project menu:
  - Compile the active file
  - Build (compile and link) modified parts of the project
  - Rebuild all elements of the project

- The last six icons (on the right) are the debugging icons. Some are duplicated in a menu item, some are not. They are discussed in more detail in Section 7 (Integrated Debugger):
  - Toggle breakpoint
  - QuickWatch view
  - Step into, step over, or step out of execution sequence

First Time VWB Entry In the Visual C++ User's Guides, VWB, pp. 14-15, a sample windows-based C++ application is shown. The sample program is named HELLO. This example uses the Microsoft Foundation Classes (MFCs) which adds to its complexity. However, proceeding through the example serves two purposes:

- It shows that the VWB has been properly installed (all systems work).
- The developer becomes familiar with VWB nomenclature.

The instructions for bringing project HELLO into the VWB, recompiling it, and executing it are:

1. Enter the VWB.

2. Pick **Project|Open** (because this is an existing project). The Open Project window appears. It allows the developer to select a project from anywhere on the hard disk. In this case project HELLO is located in directory C:\MSVC\MFC\SAMPLES.

3. In the Directories listbox, double-click on **MSVC**, then **MFC**, then **SAMPLES**, then **HELLO**. In the File Name listbox the name hello.mak appears.

Double-click on **hello.mak** and the entire project is loaded into the VWB. The loading will be successful because all the necessary files were placed into the HELLO subdirectory by the manufacturer and the paths to all the library and include files is as specified in file C:\WINDOWS\MSVC.INI.

To see which files have been loaded into the HELLO project, pick **File|Open**. The Open File window shows only two files in the listbox: hello.cpp and stdafx.cpp, where ".cpp" means C++ source language. Are there more files? You bet! At the lower left of the Open File window are the words "List Files of Type." Scroll down the list and pick **All Files**. Now a list of 24 files appears in the listbox.

HELLO.APS (Binary Resource)	HELLO.RC (Resource Script)
HELLO.BSC (Browse File Menu)	HELLO.RES (Compiled *.RC file)
HELLO.CLW (Class Wizard)	HELLO.SBR (Symb Browser Data)
HELLO.CPP (Source, C++)	HELLO.VCW (Project Status)
HELLO.DEF (Resource Defn)	HELLO.WSP (VWB Workspace Info)
HELLO.EXE (Executable Code)	MAKEFILE (Imported Make File)
HELLO.H (Header)	RESOURCE.H (Header, App Studio)
HELLO.ICO (Icon, AppStudio)	STDAFX.CPP (MFC Source, C++)
HELLO.MAK (Local Make File)	STDAFX.H (MFC, Header)
HELLO.MAP (Stack Map)	STDAFX.OBJ (MFC, Object Code)

HELLO.OBJ (Object File)   STDAFX.PCH (MFC,Pre-Comp Hdr)
HELLO.PDB (Pgm DataBase)   STDAFX.SBR (MFC, Symb. Browser)

Many of the 24 files are not editable by the developer, but they appear in the list anyway. Note that there is no provision within the VWB to delete a file. Besides the All Files option, the developer may choose one of the seven other List Files of Type settings at the bottom left of the Open File window. The file list that the writer normally needs includes source files (*.C or *.CPP), header files (*.H), resource script files (*.RC), and resource definition files (*.DEF); however this grouping is not one of the eight choices. The *.DEF file is seldom edited, but the other three (*.C, *.H, *.RC) require constant rework by the developer.

The developer may temporarily choose these types of files (to appear in the listbox) by typing the following in the single edit line below the words File Name: ***.C**; ***.H**; ***.RC**, then picking **OK**. But these choices disappear when the project is closed [Ref: User's Guides, VWB, pp. 79-81].

Fortunately, once the developer has opened and edited several files in a given project these files are listed at the bottom of the File menu window, just below the Exit menu item, and there is no requirement to pick the Open menu item repeatedly to reopen the Open Files window. Instead, the developer may pick the "last files edited" list at the bottom of the File menu window, where up to five files are listed. This feature allows the developer to open files quickly.

The compiler/linker recognizes two types of source code files, *.C (C language) and *.CPP (C++ language). A generic *.CXX is used in the Microsoft texts to show any source code privately named by the developer.

If we remove from the above list all files that are binary, symbolic (and supporting another file), or accessed solely by the AppStudio (dialog editor or graphics editor), these files remain:

- HELLO.CPP   (Source Code, C++ Language)
- HELLO.DEF   (Module Definition)
- HELLO.H   (Header)
- HELLO.RC   (Resource Script - Dialog Boxes, etc.)

In this case there is no *.DLG (dialog) file; the *.DLG data is now placed directly into the *.RC resource script file.

In this Microsoft User's Guide example no files will be edited, so the Open File window is exited by picking **Cancel**. Next, in the VWB, pick

Options|Project. Under **Build Mode** in the Project Options window, pick **Debug**, then return to the VWB main window by picking **OK**.

To recompile HELLO, pick **Project|Build HELLO.EXE**. After successful compiling and linking, the program may be executed by picking **Project|Execute HELLO.EXE**. To close the project pick **Project|Close**. To exit the VWB pick **File|Exit**.

Importing Old Projects Old project files from earlier windows-type compilers are transferable to the Visual C++ DSFW. To demonstrate this capability a project named PAYUP1 will be used (C:\MSVC\SOURCE\ BOOK1\ PAYUP1). PAYUP1 was originally written in the Programmer's Workbench in the 3.1 Software Development Kit using the C/C++ 7.0 compiler. It currently contains these files: *.MAK, *.DEF, *.C, *.RC, *.H, *.RES, *.OBJ, and *.EXE. These are the steps required to import the project into the VWB:

1. Within MS-DOS (not Windows), create a directory for the new project and copy the old files into the new directory. In the example shown here the directory has already been created and the old files have already been moved to the new directory, C:\MSVC\SOURCE\BOOK1\PAYUP1.

2. Enter Windows, and enter the VWB.

3. Pick **Project|New**. The New Project window appears. The Project Type: Windows application [.EXE] is correct.

4. The Project Name: is filled in by picking selected subdirectories in the Visual C++ system. To do this, pick **Browse**.

5. In the Browse window, in the Directories listbox, double-click on **MSVC**, then **SOURCE**, then **BOOK1**, then **PAYUP1**. The old PAYUP1.MAK filename appears in the File Name listbox but it may be "grayed" because the VWB cannot determine if it is a usable make file. Double-click on **PAYUP1.MAK** anyway.

6. The New Project window returns, and the Project Name edit box is filled with the path data to the new project. The Project Type edit box shows "Windows Application [.EXE]," which is the correct project type.

7. Pick **OK**. A new query window appears, Microsoft Visual C++, with the question, "The project C:\MSVC\SOURCE\BOOK1\PAYUP1\ PAYUP1.MAK already exists. Would you like to overwrite it?" Pick **Yes**.

The new PAYUP1 project has been formed. A new window, Edit— PAYUP1.MAK, appears. Under **List Files of Type** pick **All Files**. One new filename appears in the File Name list box, PAYUP1.VCW (the project status file). The old PAYUP1.MAK file has also been replaced with a new Visual C++ makefile.

1. Double-click on the ***.C**, ***.DEF**, and ***.RC** files in the File Name listbox to place each in the Files in Project window, the lowest box in the window. The *.H header file is considered a support file, not a project file, so it should not be placed in Files in Project. If the developer attempts to place the *.H file there anyway, the VWB presents a warning message stating that it will not be accepted as a project file, and nothing bad happens.

2. Pick **Close** to set the project files.

The main VWB window returns. To compile and execute the program:

1. Pick **Project|Build PAYUP1.EXE**.

2. A query window appears with the message, "The current project has changed. Would you like to build the affected files?" Pick **Yes**.

Every C/C++ 7.0 project includes a statement on STACKSIZE in the *.DEF file. Visual C++ does not. Therefore, a warning will appear in the output list that "both /STACK and STACKSIZE used," but the project will compile successfully anyway. This is an excellent opportunity to exercise the editing features of the VWB. This warning/error may now be corrected in the *.DEF (resource definition) file. To eliminate this warning, proceed as follows:

1. Close the output file by picking **File|Close**.

2. On the VWB main window, pick **File|Open**. In the Open File window, under List Files of Type, pick **All Files**. In the File Name listbox, pick **payup1.def** by double-clicking on it.

3. Scroll to the bottom of the PAYUP1.DEF file and delete the words "STACKSIZE 5120 ; Alternate minimum stacksize is 8192 (Petzold)." To delete this line, first highlight it using the mouse in the drag mode, then pick **Edit|Cut** at the top of the VWB window. This cuts the line out of the file.

4. In VWB pick **File|Save**. Then pick **File|Close** to close the *.DEF file.

5. In VWB pick **Project|Rebuild All PAYUP1.EXE**. The program will recompile without the STACKSIZE warning. Close the output file.

6. To execute the program, pick **Project|Execute PAYUP1.EXE**. The developer will have an opportunity to interact with this project in Section 5 of this book.

Recall that when the old PAYUP1 project was transferred into Visual C++ there were eight or nine files. During formation of the project in the VWB the *.MAK file was updated and one additional file, *.VCW (debugger status) was added. Now that the *.DEF file has been edited (to remove the STACKSIZE number) and "Rebuild All" has been exercised, there are 13 files in the PAYUP1 subdirectory! The files list includes:

- PAYUP1.DEF   (Module Definition)
- PAYUP1.H   (Header)
- PAYUP1.RC   (Resource Script)
- PAYUP1.C   (Source Code, C Language)
- PAYUP1.MAK   (Makefile)
- PAYUP1.RES   (Binary Resource File, for App Studio)
- PAYUP1.OBJ   (Object Code)
- PAYUP1.EXE   (Executable Code)
- PAYUP1.PDB   (Program Database)
- PAYUP1.SBR   (Symbolic File for Browser)
- PAYUP1.WSP   (Visual C++ Workbench Workspace Information)
- PAYUP1.BSC   (Browse File Menu)
- PAYUP1.VCW   (Status File, replacing *.STS)

Do not be concerned about the number of files that the VWB generates. The goal of the entire DSFW is to automate the development/redevelopment process such that the source of a problem may be isolated, repaired, and the project rebuilt without ever rewriting another line of executable code. This process demands extensive decomposition of what we call "source" code today into single-task elements. Each of those elements must be stored in its own file and edited by its own VWB tool. More and more of this decomposition will occur in modern software development, not less and less.

Creating New Projects with AppWizard   In this section the steps required to create a new project using AppWizard are briefly outlined. This description is taken from the User's Guides, VWB, pp. 26-27.

The AppWizard assumes that each project will contain an "about box" at the main menu entry into the application, so it creates the necessary *.RC resource script file to support both the main window menu bar and the about box. If the developer dislikes using about boxes or menu bars, the code may be easily eliminated.

The AppWizard is easy to use, but the files it produces are not. Once the developer has entered the Targetname of the project and the DOS path to the subdirectory which will share the Targetname, AppWizard does all the rest. For this exercise the Targetname will be "PAYUP0" (pronounced payup zero), and the path will be "C:\MSVC\SOURCE\BOOK1\PAYUP0." Follow these steps:

1. Enter the VWB.

2. Pick **Project|AppWizard** (the top entry).

3. The MFC AppWizard window appears. In the Project Name: edit box, type **PAYUP0**.

4. With the mouse, move to the Directory listbox, double-click on **MSVC**, then **SOURCE**, then **BOOK1**. Quit. You are finished. The path, as shown under Project Path, is: C:\MSVC\SOURCE\BOOK1\PAYUP0\ PAYUP0.MAK.

5. Pick **OK** to exit the AppWizard window. A New Application Information window appears. Pick **Create** and the project file set is formed.

The developer, with the aid of AppWizard, has now created a new subdirectory named PAYUP0 with 18 files and a subdirectory of its own named RES. This newly created project will not be used in this book.

Creating Successive Projects   This book makes good use of the capability to create a project "B" which is a clone of project "A" with small modifications. For example, project PAYUP2 is a clone of PAYUP1. There are quick methods to perform the new-project cloning process:

1. Enter MS-DOS (not Windows).

2. Create a new subdirectory for the new project. For example, if the developer decides to create a new project named PAYUP99, spawned from an old project named PAYUP2, create a subdirectory at C:\MSVC\SOURCE\BOOK1\PAYUP99.

3. Move to the PAYUP2 subdirectory and copy all files from there to subdirectory PAYUP99.

4. Move to directory PAYUP99 and rename all Payup2.* files to Payup99.*.

5. Enter MS Windows, and enter the VWB. Pick **Project|New**.

6. The New Project window appears. Pick **Browse**.

7. In the Browse window, Directories listbox, double-click on **MSVC**, then **SOURCE**, then **BOOK1**, then **PAYUP99**.

8. The file name payup99.mak is grayed in the File Name listbox because it is really file payup2.mak renamed. The VWB detects that it is an

improper makefile. Click on it twice anyway. The New Project window reappears.

9. Pick **OK** to exit the New Project window. A query message appears, "The project C: . . . . . \PAYUP99.MAK already exists. Would you like to overwrite it?" Pick **Yes**.

The new project PAYUP99 is now formed. But there are a number of inconsistencies in the source code that the developer must correct. For example, all #include statements include the wrong file names, etc. How does one find all these errors? Try compiling the project and the output file will point them out precisely.

Creating Administrative Projects   There are several opportunities to use the VWB as a simple text editor/text finder. One example is the creation of a copy of the large (82-page) include file named WINDOWS.H in a project of its own so it may be referenced and searched quickly. The developer would normally perform these types of functions within the Notepad, which is provided by MS Windows. However, Notepad cannot handle an 82-page text; it simply presents a message that "File is too large for Notepad. Use another editor to edit the file." The VWB is capable of handling large files.

The procedure listed below has already been accomplished for the developer, and file WINDLIST.DOC already resides in pseudo-project WINDLIST, at location C:\MSVC\SOURCE\WINDLIST\WINDLIST.MAK. This is how it was done:

1. Enter MS-DOS.
2. Create a new directory C:\MSVC\SOURCE\WINDLIST.
3. Copy file C:\MSVC\INCLUDE\WINDOWS.H to C:\MSVC\SOURCE\ WINDLIST\ WINDLIST.DOC.
4. Enter Windows, and the VWB.
5. Pick **Project|New**.
6. Type in the New Project window Project Name edit box: **C:\MSVC\ SOURCE\WINDLIST\WINDLIST.MAK**.
7. Pick **OK** to exit the New Project window. The Edit—WINDLIST.MAK Window appears. Exit this window by picking **Close**.
8. In the VWB, pick **File|Open**.
9. Under List Files of Type:, scroll down and pick **All Files [*.*]**.

Three files will appear in the file list box:

windlist.doc
windlist.mak
windlist.vcw

10. Pick **windlist.doc**, and it will appear in the VWB for searching, etc. The *.MAK and *.VCW files support the project only.

The windlist.doc file in project C:\MSVC\SOURCE\WINDLIST will be referred to later in the text. This same method for creating administrative projects may be used if the developer is performing documentation on a working Visual C++ project and has no word processor installed on the machine to accept the documentation text. All source code listings in the HOWPS were prepared in pseudo-projects such as "Windlist."

Preparation for Integrated Debugging   There is only one necessary setting to prepare for integrated debugging, and the developer has already set this while in the VWB Options menu:

Under Project the Build Mode was set to Debug.

This completes a brief discussion on the capabilities of the Visual C++ Workbench (VWB).

Section 3

Common Window Types

In this section the two major window types are discussed: "overlapped" and "child." Projects MAINMAIN and PAYUP in this book use only the first type, overlapped windows. Child windows are the subject of HOWPS Book 2. An excellent reference on window types is Rector 3.1, pp. 131-136.

OVERLAPPED WINDOWS

An overlapped window is always created over the top of any other screen displays—it "overlaps" any existing presentation. Overlapped windows may be linked together such that a top-level window "owns" one or more lower-tier overlapped windows, and those lower-tier overlapped windows may be further linked to even lower-tier overlapped windows that they "own." There are any number of configurations. This linking process is accomplished when each window is created. The process of window creation for the types of windows discussed in this section is shown in Figure 3-1. The top-level (main) window in any program is unowned; any other overlapped windows that appear in the program must be owned by another window—usually by the main window.

But why link the windows together during the creation process? Because the messages that control the windows operations are sent along paths of internal communication defined by the linking sequence. Some messages traverse from the owned window upward to the owner; others traverse from the owner down to the owned window.

The most notable characteristic of overlapped windows is that they are displayed on the screen totally independent of one another; each window's location and size is declared in terms of absolute screen coordinates. They may not be "nested" like child windows are, and moving an overlapped window on the screen does not cause the windows that it "owns" to move also. Therefore overlapped windows don't "stack" well either.

The Rector 3.1 and Petzold 3.1 texts define the two subgroups of overlapped windows as "overlapped" and "popup" windows, which invites nomenclature problems. For purposes of this book, we will define the two subgroups of overlapped windows as "formal windows" and "popup dialog/message boxes" to differentiate between the thick frame, formal windows and the small popups.

Overlapped Formal Windows   These are the large, top-level windows that generally have these characteristics:

- Thick frame around the window. This thick frame enables the user to resize the window by dragging the lower right corner to alternate screen positions with the mouse.
- Space for a caption (title bar) across the top of the window. If a title bar is provided, the user may move the entire window by picking the title bar and dragging the window to a new position.
- Space for a menu bar directly below the title bar. When the user picks the menu bar, a menu list is displayed in a column below the menu bar. Menu bars are unique to overlapped windows; child windows cannot have menu bars.
- May be minimized to icon size or maximized to full-screen size.
- Normally closed by picking the dashbox (System menu) at the top left corner of the window (if Windows 3.1). This produces a System menu list, and one item on the list is **Close**. Window closure is accomplished in one step in Windows 95, by picking the "**X**" box at the top right corner of the window.

Overlapped formal windows must be "registered" during program initialization. A good example of this type of window is the main window.

	Overlapped Window Type		Child Window Type
	Formal	Popup Dialog Box	
1. How each window class registered.	In WinMain( ), during initialization.	No explicit registration.	In WinMain( ), during initialization.
2. How procedure named to control window.	WndProc( ), which is named in second parameter in WNDCLASS structure during window class registration.	Procedure named in fourth argument in DialogBox( ) statement in function WndProc( ).	Any window procedure function, named in second parameter in WNDCLASS structure during class registration.
3. How each window created.	CreateWindow( ) or CreateWindowEx( ) statement.	DialogBox( ) statement, which implicitly calls CreateWindow( ) to create dialog box window.	CreateWindow( ) or CreateWindowEx( ) statement.
4. How linked to next higher-tier window.	Top-level formal window is unowned. All lower-tier formal windows are linked to (owned by) a higher-tier window by naming owner in eighth argument of CreateWindow( ) or CreateWindowEx( ) statement.	Automatically linked to top-level window. Programmer makes no direct entries into CreateWindow( ) statement.	Linked to a higher-tier formal overlapped or child window, which now becomes its parent. Parent named in eighth argument of CreateWindow( ) or CreateWindowEx( ) statement.
5. How client area filled with logic elements, text, and graphics.	By series of CreateWindow( ) statements to create logic elements, and by using GDI ** functions within case WM_PAINT.	In resource script file, *.RC.	By series of CreateWindow( ) statements to create logic elements, and by using GDI ** functions within case WM_PAINT.
6. How window top left corner specified.	Absolute screen coordinates.	Absolute screen coordinates.	With respect to position of top left corner of its parent window.

** Rector 3.1, pp 177-264.

Figure 3-1: Window types (most common usage)

Popup Dialog/Message Boxes   These are normally created for immediate use and are quickly dissipated. Popup dialog boxes are created using a DialogBox( ) or CreateDialog( ) statement, which, from the developer's viewpoint, is a far more efficient method of creating, servicing, and destroying a window than that required to perform similar tasks on a child window. DialogBox( ) creates a modal dialog box; CreateDialog( ) creates a modeless dialog box. A modal dialog box requires the immediate attention of the user since all other windows are disabled until the user attends to the box. A modeless dialog box need not be attended to by the user; it remains on the screen until the user discharges it or its usefulness is overcome by events (the program destroys it).

Dialog and message boxes are not registered at program initialization like overlapped formal windows. Instead, each dialog box is specified in the *.RC resource script file with its "template." Message boxes, which are a prepackaged subset of dialog boxes, are the easiest windows to create since they require no *.RC template; all decisions on size, shape, font, etc. are made by the compiler. The developer provides only the minimum information to create a message box—usually one or two lines of executable code. Message boxes frequently are used as a simple debugging tool during software development to display values of variables of interest on the screen.

Dialog/message boxes are normally linked to (owned by) the formal window which they overlap at creation—usually the main window. Some dialog boxes have title bars (captions) and some do not. If they have title bars they may be moved about on the screen by the user with the mouse; if they have no title bars they are fixed. Dialog boxes generally have these characteristics:

- Thinner border around the window. This thin border does not allow the user to resize the window.
- No menu bar (only overlapped formal windows have this).
- Not minimized or maximized. The min-max icons may be placed on the window if the window has a title bar, but the icons produce odd results.
- No dashbox System menu in the top left corner (Windows 3.1) or top right corner (Windows 95). The System menu may be placed on the window if the window has a title bar, but this method of closing a dialog box is seldom used.
- If "modal" type, window closure occurs when the user picks a child window control (logic element) within the popup dialog or message box. If "modeless" type, there are two ways to close the window:

- The user picks a logic element within the window (same as modal type).
- The program closes it with a DestroyWindow( ) statement when the need for the window is past (and the user has not elected to close it).

Both modal and modeless dialog boxes are required to write efficient windows programs.

If the developer has programmed using both overlapped popup and child windows, the question probably has been asked: Why do the overlapped popup (dialog box) windows *not* need the WM_PAINT case in their window controlling procedure, since WM_PAINT is such a prominent part of child windows programming? The answer is: The code written to support a dialog box (the *.RC template and the procedure that controls the window) is "rewritten" by the compiler to reorganize the presentation sequence, and this internal rewrite *does* use WM_PAINT. This is shown symbolically in Figure 3-2, Parts One and Two. Part One is sample code for a dialog box. Part Two is the pseudo-code that represents the dialog box within the program so it will handshake with all the other elements of windows programming.

CHILD WINDOWS

A totally different language is used to describe child windows and their relationship to the other elements of the program. Recall that overlapped windows are either owned or unowned, and only the main overlapped window is unowned. In the child window world the terms "child" and "parent" are used. Every child window has a parent, which means that every child window is linked to one parent window (for communications purposes, exactly as described in overlapped windows above). There may also be any number of configurations, just as with overlapped windows.

Like overlapped formal windows, child windows must be registered at program initialization. Only popups (dialog/message boxes) escape formal registration.

The most noticeable difference between overlapped and child windows is this: Every child window is displayed within the confines of its parent window. If the parent window is moved, the child moves with it. Child windows are well-ordered, and programs may be written such that if the parent window is resized by the user, then each of its child windows may be resized and redrawn along with the parent. Consequently child windows "nest" well and "stack" well.

1. Dialog Box Construct (Typical Template from PAYUP1.RC),
   Figure 5-3, lines 248-255:

```
CalcBox 6  DIALOG  50, 60, 160, 60                              A
STYLE  WS_DLGFRAME | WS_POPUP                                   B
FONT  10, "Ms Sans Serif"                                       C
  {CTEXT  "Popup #6"           -1,  0,  5, 160,  8             D
  CTEXT  "Re-Run Program ?"    -1,  0, 20, 160,  8             E
  PUSHBUTTON  "YES"       IDYES, 29, 40,  32, 14               F
  PUSHBUTTON  "NO"        IDNO, 99, 40,  32, 14                G
  }
```

2. Code from "WndProc( )", where "CalcBox6" is created and Destroyed,
   Figure 5-3, lines 401-456:

```
WndProc(HWND haWnd, UINT msg, WPARAM wParam, LPARAM lParam)
{switch(msg)
  {case WM_COMMAND:
   if(wParam == IDM_ABOUT)
     etc
   else if(wParam == IDM_CALC)
     {switch(COUNTER)
      {case 1: ...... etc
       case 6:
         lpProcCalc = MakeProcInstance(CalcProc, hInst);
         DialogBox(hInst, "CalcBox6", haWnd, lpProcCalc);        H
         FreeProcInstance(lpProcCalc);
         break;
      } /* End of switch(COUNTER) */
      break;
     }
   else /* Let windows process message */
     return(DefWindowProc(haWnd, msg, wParam lParam));
   case WM_DESTROY:
     ...... etc
  }/* End of switch(msg) */
} /* End of WndProc( ) */
```

3. Code from "CalcProc( )", the procedure controlling "CalcBox6",
   Figure 5-3, lines 601-693:

```
CalcProc(HWND haDlg, UINT msg, WPARAM wParam, LPARAM lParam)
  {switch(msg)
   {case WM_INITDIALOG:
    switch(COUNTER)
      {case 1: ...... etc
       case 6:
         return TRUE;  /* Set focus to first pushbutton */      I
      } /* End of switch(COUNTER) */
    case WM_COMMAND:
      switch(COUNTER)
        {case 1: ...... etc
         case 6: /* Re-run program ? */
           COUNTER = 1;
           if(wParam == IDYES)
             {PostMessage(ghWnd, WM_COMMAND, IDM_CALC, 0L);     J
             EndDialog(haDlg, TRUE);
             }
           return TRUE;
        } /* End of switch(COUNTER) */
      break;
   } /* End of switch(msg) */
  return FALSE;
  } /* End of CalcProc( ) */
```

Figure 3-2 Part One: Developer-written dialog box code

1. Pseudo internal "WndProc( )" type code, where "CalcBox6" is both created and destroyed.

```
switch(msg)
  {case WM_COMMAND:
    if(wParam == IDM_ABOUT)
      etc
    if(wParam == IDM_CALC)
      {switch(COUNTER)
        {case 1: ...... etc
        case 6:
          hFontCalc6 = CreateFont(font size + 10 parameters that
            describe font "MS Sans Serif" );

          Ptr6 = CreateWindow(DIALOG, NULL, WS_DLGFRAME | WS_POPUP,
                          50, 60, 160, 60, hWnd, NULL, hInst, NULL);
          /* Create YES and NO pushbuttons */
          Ptr6-1 = CreateWindow(BUTTON,"YES",
                          WS_CHILDWINDOW | WS_BORDER | WS_VISIBLE,
                          29, 40, 32, 14, Ptr6, IDYES, hInst, NULL);
          Ptr6-2 = CreateWindow(BUTTON, "NO",
                          WS_CHILDWINDOW | WS_BORDER | WS_VISIBLE,
                          99, 40, 32, 14, Ptr6, IDNO, hInst, NULL);

          /* Send font to pushbuttons */
          SendMessage(Ptr6-1, WM_SETFONT, hFontCalc6, 0L);

          SendMessage(Ptr6-2, WM_SETFONT, hFontCalc6, 0L);

          break;
        } /* End of switch(COUNTER) */
      break;
      }
    else /* Let windows process message */
      return(DefWindowProc(haWnd, msg, wParam lParam));

  case WM_DESTROY:
    ...... etc
  }/* End of switch(msg) */
```

2. Pseudo internal "CalcProc( )" type code:

```
switch(msg)
  {caseWM_PAINT: /* Put text or graphics onto dialog box */
    hdc = BeginPaint( );
    SelectObject(hdc, hFontCalc6); /* Install proper font */
    SetTextAlign(hdc, TA_CENTER);
    TextOut(hdc, 5, 160, "Popup #6", 8 chars);
    SetTextAlign(hdc, TA_CENTER);
    TextOut(hdc, 20, 160, "Re-Run Program ?", 16 chars);
    /* YES and NO pushbuttons become visible here */
    EndPaint( );
    SetFocus( ); /* Set focus to pushbutton */
    return 0;
  case WM_COMMAND: /* Response after pushbutton depressed */
    switch(COUNTER)
      {case 1: ...... etc
      case 6: /* Re-run program ? */
        COUNTER = 1;
        if(wParam == IDYES)
          {PostMessage(ghWnd, WM_COMMAND, IDM_CALC, 0L);
          EndDialog(haDlg, TRUE);
          }
        return TRUE;
      } /* End of switch(COUNTER) */
    break;
  } /* End of switch(msg) */
```

Figure 3-2 Part Two: Pseudo 3.1 compiler code

Child windows may be endowed with most of the characteristics of overlapped formal windows, to include a System menu (left dashbox or right "X"), a caption (title bar), or even minimize/maximize icons if the title bar is included in the window. If the thick frame is used, the window may be resized by the user with the mouse. However, child windows cannot have a menu bar, which appears on an overlapped window directly below the title bar. [See Rector 3.1, p. 135.]

QUESTION: Why no menu bar?

ANSWER: The ninth parameter in a CreateWindow( ) statement is a challenge to new developers because it accomplishes two completely different tasks in overlapped formal windows and child windows. [Recall that there is no Parameter #9 in overlapped popup window creation because there is no explicit CreateWindow( ) statement.]

The compiler determines whether the window creation will be type WS_OVERLAPPED or WS_CHILD when Parameter #3 in the argument list is read. Therefore the compiler is able to decipher the dual meaning of Parameter #9 which follows.

In overlapped formal windows creation, Parameter #9 is always shown as "NULL;" it is a simple space filler. Since the window type is WS_OVERLAPPED, the symbolic name of its menu bar (as entered in the *.RC template) is taken from the window registration "wc.lpszMenuName" value in WinMain( ). If the wc.lpszMenuName is also "NULL" this means that no menu bar is required on this overlapped formal window. Since "NULL" always occupies Parameter #9 this argument cannot be used to designate a unique ID for an overlapped formal window. Consequently the only method for accessing this type of window is through its assigned handle name. For this reason overlapped formal window handle names are usually declared globally (more explanation follows in later HOWPS books).

If Parameter #3 in the CreateWindow( ) statement is type WS_CHILD, then the compiler accepts Parameter #9 as a unique ID for the window. If no unique ID is required, then "NULL" is placed there; in this case "NULL" does *not* mean "go to wc.lpszMenuName in the window registration and read the menu bar symbolic name" since child windows cannot have menu bars. However, most child windows *do* require a unique ID because this is the *only* way a child window may be accessed when the child window is placed into a dialog box. To state it another way, the success of the entire dialog box/dialog *.RC template scheme rests on the ability of the program to access child windows within a dialog box with their unique IDs; their window handle names are inaccessible.

QUESTION: What type of child windows are we talking about?

ANSWER: That subset of child windows known as "child window controls," which are predefined logic elements such as pushbuttons, radiobuttons, checkboxes, editboxes, etc. Each of these elements is a child window, and each must be assigned a unique ID to be accessed once they are placed within their "parent" window, which may be a dialog box, an overlapped formal window, or a higher-tier child window.

QUESTION: What is meant by "accessing the child window"?

ANSWER: Logic elements (pre-defined child window controls) are "accessed" to put data onto and take data off dialog boxes, overlapped formal windows, and higher-tier child windows. The edit control, for example, is "accessed" to accept keyboard input from the user and place the input into an ASCII string until the program can act upon it.

Since only one parameter space has been provided for both menu bars and unique IDs, any given window can have only one of the two. Overlapped formal windows have the menu bar (and no unique ID); child windows have the unique ID (and no menu bar).

QUESTION: What is wrong with having both?

ANSWER: Not sure. This was a Visual C++ architectural decision made long ago. However, child windows generally do not need menu bars. But it would be handy if overlapped formal windows had unique IDs so their handle names could be "retrieved" easily. As stated earlier, since overlapped formal windows do not have unique IDs, their handle names should be declared globally—the handle name is the only way to access the window. Conversely, since all child windows may be assigned unique IDs in Parameter #9, they may be assigned either local or global handle names which are easily retrievable within the program. A discussion of window handle name retrieval is included in HOWPS Book 2.

According to Rector 3.1, p. 134, "Child windows are used more frequently than any other type of window. Whereas there might be only a few overlapped or popup windows created at any given time, there are most likely tens, if not hundreds, of child windows in existence." But there is an "Achilles heel" in child windows programming. Petzold 3.1, p. 208 states it this way: "Using child window controls directly on the surface of your [child or overlapped formal] window involves tasks of a lower level than are required for using child window controls in a dialog box [an overlapped, popup window], where the dialog box manager adds a layer of insulation between your program and the controls themselves. In particular, you'll discover that the child window controls you create on the surface of your [child or overlapped formal] window have no built-in facility to move the input focus from one control to another using the Tab or cursor movement keys. A child window control [logic element] can obtain the focus, but once it does, it won't relinquish the input focus back to the parent window."

Whenever the HOWPS uses the term "child window" it refers to those windows which:

- Are created explicitly in the source code with CreateWindow( ) or CreateWindowEx( ) statements.
- Require that a window controlling procedure be included in the project source code, and
- Are **not** child window controls (logic elements).

This definition excludes those precoded elements such as pushbuttons, radiobuttons, checkboxes, edit controls, listboxes, comboboxes, scrollbar controls, etc., which are commonly called "child window controls." The terms "child windows" and "child window controls" are so similar that they lose their identities. The HOWPS will use terms "child windows" and "logic elements" instead, to keep them separated.

The HOWPS uses the term "dialogs" to mean child windows which have logic elements on them; they perform the same function as dialog boxes in the child window world. The term "dialog boxes" will always mean those windows which are created with DialogBox( ) or CreateDialog( ), have type BOOL window controlling procedures, and have templates in the *.RC resource script file.

Another way to state the differences between overlapped popup dialog boxes and child windows is this: Dialog boxes begin with a "template" and code similar to that found in Figure 3-2, Part One. Child windows require coding similar to the pseudo-code found in Figure 3-2, Part Two. Coding for child windows is more primitive than coding for dialog boxes, but the more primitive coding allows more flexibility in the window display. For example, all text in a dialog box must be displayed in the same font and font size. In a child window each line of text may be displayed with a different font and font size. However this increased capability takes additional developer time to prepare.

The developer will soon discover that the most convenient form of window below the main window level, a child window with dialog box attributes, does not exist. Since the intent of this first book is to introduce the developer to simplified windows programming, child windows are not used in the first two projects in this book. Project MAINMAIN uses one overlapped formal main window; project PAYUP uses one overlapped formal main window and a series of eight overlapped popup dialog boxes and two popup message boxes to conduct program logic.

Project MAINMAIN

Project MainMain is provided as a starting point for windows programming. It includes a main window Begin menu with two menu items:

> About MainMain
> Start MainMain

The word *Begin* appears on a menu bar which is directly below the caption (title bar). When menu item Start MainMain is picked, one line of text appears, underlined, in the center of the main window. The window may be moved by picking the title bar and dragging it to a new location on the screen, or the window may be increased or decreased in size by dragging the lower-right corner with the mouse. Then the text may be repainted on the screen by picking Start MainMain again.

The individual components of the project are outlined below.

ABOUT BOX

Nearly every windows application has an "AboutBox." It is always an overlapped window of the popup dialog box type. It contains information on the application's copyright. Because the AboutBox is so common, the AppWizard tool in the VWB creates one at the onset of every new application.

The template for the AboutBox appears in the *.RC resource script file. If the developer uses no other dialog boxes in the application, the presence of the AboutBox alone will dictate the need for the *.RC file. To go one step farther, most AboutBoxes are accessed through a main window menu. The main window menu is always described in the same *.RC template file where the AboutBox description is found. Therefore, so long as new projects are started within the VWB using AppWizard, every application will contain the main window menu and the AboutBox, both of which are described in file *.RC.

STARTING THE PROGRAM

Every program must have a starting point. Most applications choose to include the main window menu with a title like "Begin," as shown above with two or more menu items on the list. One of those menu items is normally the AboutBox; the other starts the program. By placing the Start MainMain menu item on the main window menu, the user is given the capability to recycle the program from the main window. Without this option the program must be terminated each time and then re-executed by the user after each cycle.

There can be only one menu bar on the main window; it appears directly below the title bar in the window. Each individual menu item in the main window menu may have submenu items that appear when that menu item is picked. The menu item's submenu items always appear to the right of the original menu item and are said to be "cascaded." The layout for cascaded menus is determined in the *.RC template file also. If multiple, separate menus are required on a window they may appear on free-floating menus, which are discussed in Book 6.

Some applications move directly to a second window as soon as the main window is opened, perhaps using a timer to display the main window for a short period of time before overwriting it with the first application-unique window. When this is done, the main window Begin menu and its menu items are not included because they are bypassed and are inaccessible to the user.

The start-up options for a windows program are:

- If the program should be recyclable for re-execution of the program sequence, the main window menu approach is used.
- If program recycling is not required, the developer may choose to enter the program sequence directly, with no intervening move by the user (bypassing the main window menu).

The two startup techniques will be demonstrated on the second project series, PAYUP; MAINMAIN will be kept as simple as possible.

NECESSARY PROJECT FILES

The four most common windows files, *.DEF, *.H., *.RC, and *.C, are explained below:

Module Definition File (*.DEF)   This file defines a series of mandatory option settings for the linker: EXETYPE, STUB, CODE, DATA, and HEAPSIZE. In previous versions of the MS "C" compilers a STACKSIZE declaration was also required here but is no longer required. One other item, EXPORTS, is also shown here by some developers but may be deferred to individual declarations at each "exportable" function. Petzold 3.1 does not include a list of EXPORTS here; Rector 3.1 does. For our purposes, "_export" will be declared at each exportable function header and at the prototype declarations at the top of the *.C source code. Therefore, a list of exportable functions is not required in the *.DEF file.

The NAME and DESCRIPTION entries are there for the developer's use. STUB is important when a user attempts to execute the program outside of windows. It tells the user that the program is executable only within Windows.

There is no reason to change CODE, DATA, and HEAPSIZE entries, unless the developer generates much larger programs in the future. The most important item, STACKSIZE, is now computed internally by the compiler to relieve the developer of this chore.

Header File (*.H)   This file is required to set the define statements for both the manually-generated resource script (*.RC) file and the main body of code written by the developer, the *.C file. In many cases the header file is small and the developer may be tempted to copy it into both the *.RC and *.C files at the onset of the project, which negates the need to include it in the project scheme. This is not good practice because it provides one more place where an error in project declarations can occur (for example, the define statements may be changed in *.RC, but not in *.C).

When the AppStudio Dialog Editor is used to add or change menus or dialog boxes to an existing application, a second header file, RESOURCE.H, is generated by the Dialog Editor to define integer values for the subcomponents of the new or edited menu/dialog box components. The developer must include this second header file at the top of the original *.H header file.

When the entire contents of the *.RC file are created originally in the AppStudio Dialog Editor the RESOURCE.H file may be the only header file required in the project (since it contains all the define information for the entire project). In this case the *.H file is omitted, but the RESOURCE.H file must be included in the *.C file, in place of the usual "#include *.H" statement. RESOURCE.H is automatically included in a *.RC file created or edited within the Dialog Editor.

Resource Script File (*.RC)   This file contains a description of the main window menu (if used), the About Box, and each of the popup dialog boxes used in the project. The descriptions are called "templates" and may be manually created by editing the *.RC file in the VWB or created within the AppStudio Dialog Editor, which automates many of the resource script file functions. Initial construction of dialog boxes is better performed within the Dialog Editor because the process automatically creates the necessary "#define" statements that must appear in the accompanying RESOURCE.H file. If a developer creates new dialog box templates by editing, copying, and pasting within the *.RC file, care must be taken to include any new definitions in the RESOURCE.H file since the Dialog Editor has no interaction in the manual creation/editing process.

Source Code File (*.C)   This is the collection of developer-written C language source code functions. It includes:

- The entry point into a windows program, WinMain( ). All window class registrations occur here.
- A procedure that controls the main window, WndProc( ). Most lower-tier windows are created in this procedure also.
- A procedure to control each additional dialog box or child window (or each *group* of dialog boxes or child windows). Such a procedure may control either dialog boxes or child windows, but no one procedure can control both types. A procedure controlling a window must be type **long**; a procedure controlling a dialog box must be type **BOOL**.
- Other procedures to perform ancillary functions such as printing, computation, file management, etc.

The linkage of these file types is shown in Figure 4-1. There are many other files generated by a project within the VWB, especially when the Microsoft Foundation Class (MFC) option is used, which provide permanent storage for the data generated by the VWB tools in behalf of the project. However, these files are of no interest at this time.

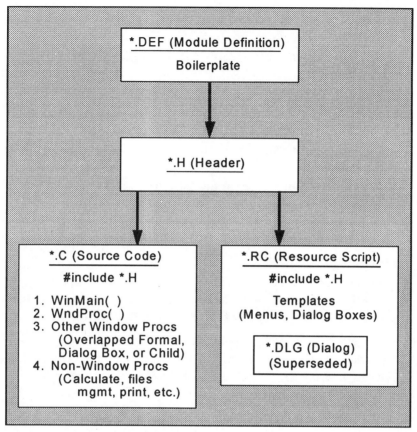

Figure 4-1: Developer-edited project files

EXPERIMENTING WITH MAINMAIN

The purpose of this project is to demonstrate:

- The standard sequence of events within a window program.

- The difference achieved in window performance when the WinMain( ) window class registration declaration in parameter "wc.style" is "NULL" versus "CS_VREDRAW | CS_HREDRAW."

- The parameters within a main window style declaration in WndProc( ), which is part of its CreateWindow( ) statement, argument #3, that allow the main window to be:

- **Closed or moved** by picking the System menu dashbox at the top left corner of the window.

- **Initially "fixed" or "movable" on the display screen.** Any window which includes a WS_CAPTION (title bar) style is movable on the screen. The user picks the title bar to drag the window to a new location. If no WS_CAPTION style, the top left corner of the window is fixed in its originally created position.

- **Initially positioned and sized** by selected window creation parameters or by default windows system choices.

- **Maximized (full-screen) or minimized (icon) in size** by the user after its initial display.

- Initially maximizing a main window by including parameter SW_SHOWMAXIMIZED in the main window's ShowWindow( ) statement in WinMain( ).

- The interdependence of the WS_CAPTION (title bar) style, WS_SYSMENU (System menu dashbox) style, the WS_THICK FRAME style, and the WS_MINIMIZEBOX | WS_MAXIMIZEBOX styles.

The commonly used window styles which appear in argument #3 in the CreateWindow( ) or CreateWindowEx( ) statement are summarized in Figure 4-2. The decisions the developer must make about the form and capabilities of the main window are shown in this figure:

- **Style WS_CAPTION** This is the most important decision the developer makes. Including this style guarantees that some type of border will be placed around the window, it will have a title bar, and it will be movable by the user with the mouse. If this style is omitted, the window's upper-left corner location on the screen is fixed. In addition, failure to choose style WS_CAPTION means that styles WS_SYSMENU, WS_MINIMIZEBOX, and WS_MAXIMIZEBOX may not be used on the window.

- **Style WS_SYSMENU** This style places a dashbox (System menu) at the top left corner of the window (if Windows 3.1), or an "X" at the top right corner of the window (if Windows 95). When the dash is picked by the user a menu list is displayed that includes options to Close the window, Move the window, etc. This is always a cumbersome two-pick move. In Windows 95, picking the "X" closes the window immediately, with only one pick. WS_SYSMENU cannot be used without WS_CAPTION.

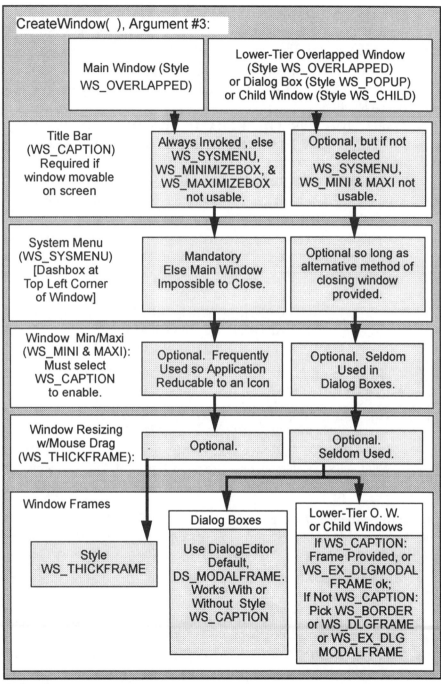

Figure 4-2: Common window styles

- **Styles WS_MINIMIZEBOX and WS_MAXIMIZEBOX** are invoked to allow the user to minimize (reduce to icon size) and maximize (full screen) a window. They cannot be used without WS_CAPTION.

- **Style WS_THICKFRAME** is invoked to allow the user to resize the window by dragging its lower-right corner with the mouse to a new screen location.

- **Frame styles WS_THICKFRAME, WS_BORDER, WS_DLG-FRAME, WS_EX_DLGMODALFRAME, and DS_MODALFRAME** As Figure 4-2 shows:

  - Style WS_THICKFRAME is usually reserved for the main window, or any window that requires resizing during program execution.

  - Styles WS_BORDER and WS_DLGFRAME are used for all other windows. However, they are redundant if style WS_CAPTION is included in argument #3. For example, all four style declarations shown below produce the same frame with a caption:

    WS_CAPTION
    WS_CAPTION | WS_BORDER
    WS_CAPTION | WS_DLGFRAME
    WS_CAPTION | WS_BORDER | WS_DLGFRAME

    If there is no title bar (WS_CAPTION), styles WS_BORDER and WS_DLGFRAME produce different window frames.

  - Style DS_MODALFRAME is reserved for dialog boxes only. It is the default frame used in the AppStudio Dialog Editor.

  - Style WS_EX_DLGMODALFRAME is used with the Create WindowEx( ) statement only [Rector 3.1, p. 344]. This frame may be used either with or without a title bar (WS_CAPTION).

Standard Sequence of Events A listing of the *.DEF, *.H, *.RC, and *.C files in project MainMain is shown in Figure 4-3, page 73, at the end of this section. The project sequence is explained below. The four necessary files are:

- **MAINMAIN.DEF** The module definition file is shown as lines 001-010.

- **MAINMAIN.H** The header file is shown as lines 101-103. This file is included in both the files that follow (*.RC and *.C).

- **MAINMAIN.RC** The resource script file, is shown as lines 201-217. This file contains a description of the main window menu and the AboutBox. The description of the AboutBox within MAINMAIN.RC is referred to as a "template." For now the template is prepared in advance for the developer; later the developer will be expected to create the template initially using the AppStudio Dialog Editor tool, which is accessible from the VWB. Once the template is initially created the developer has the choice of returning to the Dialog Editor for re-work of the template or editing it directly in the *.RC file.

- **MAINMAIN.C** This is the collection of developer-written source code functions. They include:

  - All global declarations, lines 301-316. Line 302, "define STRICT," invokes an expanded set of definitions within file WINDOWS.H, which is the main mapping file between code that the developer sees and code that is unseen but very much active in the program. The STRICT definition always comes *before* the "#include <windows.h>" statement in any windows project [Rector 3.1, p. 42]. WINDOWS.H is an ASCII file, and if dumped to the printer is about 80 pages long. If the developer elects to peruse this file, the text editor provided in MS Windows named Notepad cannot handle it (the file is too large). However the copy of WINDOWS.H made earlier in project C:\MSVC\SOURCE\WINDLIST and renamed WINDLIST.DOC is accessible for viewing within the VWB.

    Later the developer may choose to exclude portions of the WINDOWS.H file in selected projects to save space. For more information about this, see Rector 3.1, pp. 31-36.

    The function prototypes are shown in lines 306-307, and include the "_export" statement. Any discussion of the meaning of EXPORT and its companion CALLBACK will be deferred to later books. One immediate reference is Rector 3.1, pp. 26, 29-30, 104-107, and 565. A procedure that controls a dialog box will always be type "BOOL;" a procedure that controls any other type of window will be type "long."

  - WinMain( ), the entry point for project MAINMAIN [and all windows programs]. WinMain( ) in this project is a collection of three functions normally separated by Rector 3.1: WinMain( ), InitApplication( ), and InitInstance( ). Petzold 3.1 has elected to place all three in WinMain( ), and this book follows his lead. Later, as the developer's programs become more complex, the Rector 3.1 formulation may be beneficial from the standpoint of saving region, stack space, etc. in the executable program since the initialization functions may be discarded soon after program execution begins.

- WndProc( ), the highest-level window procedure. This procedure is named in WinMain( ) to be the recipient of all main window message traffic. Nearly every message passes through WndProc( ) first; if a message is not processed there it is passed to a default window procedure, DefWindowProc( ), which has access to the multitude of macros included in the windows installation (line 457).

- AboutProc( ) is the procedure that controls the AboutBox in the project (lines 501-513).

Main Window Construct and the Main Message Loop   The main window is the first item described in WinMain( ). A WNDCLASS structure is filled with 10 parameters to describe what the main window should look like (lines 324-334). Then the window class is registered for later use. More than one window could use this window class in the program, but there is only one main window, so it is uniquely defined.

Struct WNDCLASS wc;

Parameter No.	Description
1.	wc.style = NULL; /* or CS_VREDRAW I CS_HREDRAW */
2.	wc.lpfnWndProc = WndProc;
3.	wc.cbClsExtra = 0;
4.	wc.cbWndExtra = 0;
5.	wc.hInstance = hInstance;
6.	wc.hIcon = LoadIcon(NULL, IDI_APPLICATION);
7.	wc.hCursor = LoadCursor(NULL, IDC_ARROW);
8.	wc.hbrBackground = GetStockObject(WHITE_BRUSH);
9.	wc.lpszMenuName = "MainMainMenu";
10.	wc.lpszClassName = "MainMainWClass";

The important parameters are:

- **Parameter #1**, which sets the window *class* style, [window class style is set here; individual window styles are set in the individual CreateWindow( ) statements that follow]. For purposes of this book and most that follow, the two principal class styles will be "NULL" and "CS_VREDRAW | CS_HREDRAW," where the vertical line represents the bitwise OR operator. HREDRAW and VREDRAW stand for horizontal and vertical redraw. A complete listing of the 13 window class styles is in WINDLIST.DOC, under "#define CS_," or Rector 3.1, pp. 128-131.

- NULL is the default class style, since it commands no automatic repainting of the screen when main window size changes. Most programs work sufficiently well with class style "NULL." When the developer chooses the NULL class style, the windows system issues a WM_SIZE message to WndProc( ) at initial window creation and each time the user resizes the window, but no WM_PAINT message is issued to repaint the main window. It becomes the program's responsibility to reset any variable-sized child windows text or graphics on the main window and manually repaint the window.

- When the CS_VREDRAW | CS_HREDRAW class style is selected, any change in window size causes both the WM_SIZE and WM_PAINT messages to be issued by the windows system to WndProc( ).

Which is the preferred case? In Project MAINMAIN, using style CS_VREDRAW | CS_HREDRAW conveniently clears the main window whenever its size is changed, whereas style NULL commands no repaint and the main window becomes cluttered. Therefore, in this simple demonstration the CS_VREDRAW | CS_HREDRAW is the preferred style (over the NULL style).

The situation may switch, however (and NULL become the preferred style), if there are complex child windows painted on the main window and those child windows must be immediately redrawn when main window size changes.

Why would NULL be the preferred class style in this case? The change in size of the main window causes a WM_SIZE message to be sent to WndProc( ), which may be used to initiate the recomputation of child window layouts. Meanwhile, if the style is CS_VREDRAW | CS_HREDRAW, then a WM_PAINT message is also sent to WndProc( ), and the repaint may be executed *before* the recomputation is accomplished! This is demonstrated in Book 2, *Child Windows*, Project CHILDTEM, where the NULL style is used to preclude automatic repainting of the main window when its size is changed.

These two class styles, NULL and CS_VREDRAW | CS_HREDRAW, are demonstrated in MAINMAIN. The developer must change the "wc.style = " setting and recompile the project to try both styles.

- **Parameter #2**, which names a procedure, WndProc( ) to retrieve all messages for this main window. Many windows may be created later using this class registration, but they *all* must use the same window controlling procedure, WndProc( ).

- **Parameter #5**, which provides an instance number for this copy of the application. This allows multiple copies of a program to be operating on the same CPU. This instance number is assigned at the start of program execution and is used everywhere in the program. Microsoft likes to place this number, hInstance, into a global variable "hInst" immediately after registration of the main window, and uses it from that global source (line 340).

- **Parameter #9**, which names the menu resource which will appear in the resource definition file, MAINMAIN.RC, to describe its main window menu. Windows provides for only one menu bar for each overlapped formal window. The main window is the only overlapped formal window in the project, and the symbolic name for its menu bar appears in this registration. By placing the name "MainMainMenu" in this parameter, line 333, the decision is made that *if* a main window menu bar is used in this window, its template name will be MainMainMenu. If no MainMainMenu template appears in the MAINMAIN.RC file, then no menu bar will appear in the main window display below the title bar, and no error message will be shown at project compilation and linking to show that a menu bar is missing (provided for in the registration but never implemented in the *.RC file).

  If this registration was other than an overlapped formal window class, this parameter would be shown as "NULL."

TIP: In the CreateWindow( ) discussion that follows later, a window style **WS_SYSMENU** will appear frequently. This window style has *absolutely nothing to do* with the naming of a main window menu bar in Parameter #9. What WS_SYSMENU does is create a means of closing or moving a window by placing a dashbox at the top left corner of the window (Windows 3.1) or an "X" at the top right corner of the window (Windows 95). Do not confuse the WS_SYSMENU menu with the "main window menu bar" which is created from a template in the *.RC resource script file and is displayed directly below the title bar of an overlapped window.

QUESTION: Does the developer have the option to register yet another overlapped formal window, name a menu resource in its Parameter #9 declaration, then create such a window later with a menu bar that is described in a menu template in the *.RC file?

ANSWER: Yes, but a menu bar is seldom used below the main window level.

- **Parameter #10**, which names the window class. This name will be used every time this class of window is created. Since this is the main window, it will be created only one time.

The last statement after the declaration of the 10 parameters is the registration statement, line 335. At this point the main window structure is registered. (Petzold 3.1, p. 29, or Rector 3.1, pp. 59 & 68.)

Lines 336-337 are not required in any project. They post an error message on the screen if the main window registration fails.

TIP: If the developer finds it necessary to use a MessageBox( ) statement before the main window is opened, the first argument in the statement, which is the handle of the owner of the message box, must be "NULL," meaning that the owner of the message box is the Windows desktop. After the main window is opened, its handle may be used as the first argument in the Message Box statement. Do not use "NULL" for the first argument after the main window is displayed, since it makes it difficult to destroy the window later.

What is window registration all about? The most important accomplishments of a registration are:

- The procedure that will control the window class is named in Parameter #2.
- If this is a main window registration and if the main window will use a menu bar, then the menu's template name is declared in Parameter #9.
- The window class's name is declared in Parameter #10. This window class name is the sole registration "link" to any window(s) created later.

Notice what a window registration *does not* accomplish:

- No location on the screen or window size is set.
- No internal communication system is declared (naming the parent/child/owner of the window).

- No detailed attributes of the window are declared [should it have a caption (title bar), a menu bar, a thin or thick frame, should it be capable of shrinking to icon size, etc.].

All of the above details are left to the window creation statement(s). Several windows may be created later from one window registration, *but* they must all share the same window controlling procedure (Parameter #2). As a result, each significant window created in a project usually has its own registration class so it may possess its own unique window controlling procedure.

In MAINMAIN main window creation begins with line 342. A global pointer of type HWND named "ghWnd" is assigned to the main window. The CreateWindow( ) statement, line 342, has 11 arguments [Petzold 3.1, p. 32, or Rector 3.1, pp. 70 - 74]:

- **Arg #1** "MainMainWClass," the name of the registered window class above, Parameter #10.

- **Arg #2** "MainMain Application," the text for the window title bar. This entry must be enabled by entering window style WS_CAPTION in **Arg #3** below.

- **Arg #3** WS_OVERLAPPEDWINDOW, the window style (Rector 3.1, pp. 131 - 145). There are 28 window styles (see WINDLIST.DOC and search on "#define WS_"). The most important main window style, WS_OVERLAPPEDWINDOW, is defined to be WS_OVERLAPPED | WS_CAPTION | WS_SYSMENU | WS_THICKFRAME | WS_MINIMIZEBOX | WS_MAXIMIZEBOX. This window style services most main windows since it is all-inclusive. These are window styles which are declared during main window creation, not to be confused with window *class* style(s) which are declared during window registration.

If this was a child window creation statement, the style WS_OVERLAPPEDWINDOW would be replaced by WS_CHILD or WS_CHILDWINDOW. Style WS_CHILD/WS_CHILDWINDOW is a primitive style and incorporates no WS_CAPTION, WS_SYSMENU, WS_MINIMIZEBOX, or WS_MAXIMIZEBOX styles since these styles seldom appear in child windows. The one common style that appears in both overlapped and child windows is style WS_CAPTION; all windows may have a title bar. Recall that if style WS_CAPTION is included then the window is movable; if no WS_CAPTION then the window's top left corner is fixed.

- **Arg #4** CW_USEDEFAULT, the default horizontal position of the top left corner of the main window. Coordinate X increases as the window moves to the right on the screen.

- **Arg #5** CW_USEDEFAULT, the default vertical position of the top left corner of the main window. Coordinate Y increases as the window moves down on the screen.

- **Arg #6** CW_USEDEFAULT, the default width of the main window.

- **Arg #7** CW_USEDEFAULT, the default height of the main window.

- **Arg #8** NULL, indicates that this window has no parent or owner window. If this was a child window creation or a lower-tier overlapped window creation, the pointer "handle" to the window's parent or owner would be shown here. Only the main window creation statement may have a "NULL" entry here.

- **Arg #9** NULL, indicates that the main window menu *.RC template whose name appears in Parameter #9 in the window class registration above should be used to create a menu bar on this window. "NULL" appears in Arg #9 in all overlapped formal window creations.

  QUESTION: Can a menu bar be created within a child window, just below its title bar?

  ANSWER: No. See Section 2 in this book.

- **Arg #10** hInstance, indicates that this instance number owns this copy of this main window. The program could have used the global "hInst" here.

- **Arg #11** NULL, indicates that no additional pointer is needed for this window (this is an extra item used in advanced programming).

The developer may choose to alter these arguments to better fit the desired final product on advanced projects, but for now these main window defaults will suffice.

The CreateWindow( ) statement initiates several messages that are routed to the main window controlling procedure, WndProc( ) [Ref. *Windows 3.1 Programmer's Reference, Volume 2*, p. 132] to provide for computations and setups that may be required later in the project. Included in these messages is a WM_SIZE message. The WM_SIZE message is sent to WndProc( ) initially at window creation and every time thereafter when window size changes. WndProc( ) processes the WM_SIZE message in lines 448-453, and global variables StartX and StartY are computed. These values are required in the main window paint statement, lines 429-442, which are executed after boolean variable START is set to TRUE (it is FALSE at project startup).

The CreateWindow( ) statement also initiates a one-time WM_CREATE message that is sent to WndProc( ), is trapped at line 423, and a large font is created for use in writing on the main window later. Case WM_CREATE in WndProc( ) is used primarily for two purposes:

- Compute global variables that are unchanged throughout project execution.
- Create lower-tier windows whose owner or parent will be the main window and the windows need be created only once. Once the user recycles the project the WM_CREATE case is no longer automatically accessible (since it is called only at main window creation). These lower-tier window creations are also performed under the WM_ COMMAND case, which *is* accessible after project recycling.

Experimenting with Initial Main Window Location   Lines 342, 343, and 344 are the same main window creation statement, repeated three times:

- Line 342 is the standard window creation statement, where Create Window( ) parameters 4-7 are named as "CW_USEDEFAULT." This allows the windows system to choose the starting point of the main window (the top-left corner) and the window size, so the window appears at an arbitrary place on the screen. Note that all the styles that make up style "WS_OVERLAPPEDWINDOW" are individually listed in this line for later testing on this project.
- Line 343 assigns specific dimensions for the top left corner (X coordinate = 1, Y coordinate = 60, window width = 600, and window height = 400). This combination of numbers places the window originally at the same location each time the project is executed.
- Line 344 assigns a specific dimension for the X coordinate, floats the Y coordinate, and fixes the window width and length. This combination *will not work.*

At this point the main window style has been registered and a handle ghWnd has been assigned to the main window. But the window is not yet visible. Lines 346-349 make the main window visible. The normal "ShowWindow( )" statement is line 346. However, if the developer chooses to open the main window *maximized*, then line 348 should be used.

The only element remaining in WinMain( ) is the main message loop, which will control all aspects of the program until the program is terminated (lines 350-352).

About Box Construct and Sequencing MAINMAIN's AboutBox is set one level below the main window menu, in Begin. The linkage of this main menu bar Begin to the main window is determined when the main window class is registered (line 335). The symbolic menu name is "MainMainMenu, line 333," and this symbolic name must appear in the resource script file, MAINMAIN.RC, where the menu bar is described (line 204). In line 205 the ampersand in front of the word "Begin" forces the "B" to be underlined on the main window, and the menu may be opened by either pressing **Alt+B** or picking the word **Begin** with the mouse.

Once the main menu has been opened the two menu items appear:

> About MainMain
> Start MainMain

To invoke the AboutBox, the user either presses **Alt+A** or picks **About MainMain** with the mouse. This action generates a WM_COMMAND message which is sent to the procedure that controls the main window, WndProc( ) as its second argument. WndProc( ), along with every other windows procedure, has four arguments:

WndProc(HWND haWnd,UINT msg, WPARAM wParam, LPARAM lParam);

- **Argument #1** A pointer (handle) to this window.
- **Argument #2** A message (WM_COMMAND in this case).
- **Argument #3** The wParam value, which indicates the routing of the message once it enters the procedure that controls the window. The wParam value in this case is IDM_ABOUT, which is the symbolic name assigned to the "About MainMain" menu item within the MAINMAIN.RC resource script file (line 206). Windows cannot operate with the symbolic name (integers are required), so IDM_ABOUT is defined in MAINMAIN.H (line 102) as the integer 10.
- **Argument #4** The lParam value, which is a further message router value, if needed. In this case lParam is not used and is set to zero.

If WM_COMMAND is found in the message "msg" cases in WndProc( ) it is processed there. If not, the message is passed to DefWindowProc( ) for processing by other windows macros (line 457). In this case WM_COMMAND is located within WndProc( ), at line 409. Because wParam is assigned the value IDM_ABOUT, lines 410-415 are executed next.

Up to this point the procedure that governs the use of the AboutBox, AboutProc( ), has not been given a handle so it can be executed. Line 411 assigns a "far pointer" handle to the procedure, and line 412 creates the About dialog box. The second argument in line 412 is the only mention of the symbolic name of the About Box template in the MAINMAIN.RC resource script file.

Lines 210-217 in file *.RC are the template which describes the About Dialog Box. The word DIALOG identifies the script as a dialog box (the only other type of script is the MENU). The four numbers on line 210 specify the location of the top left corner of the dialog box and its dimensions (width, length):

- The box is displaced 22 units to the right of the left edge of the screen.
- The box is displaced 17 units down from the top of the client area of the main window.
- The box width is 110 units.
- The box height is 55 units.

But what is a "unit"? This will be discussed in "Popup Dialog Boxes" in Section 5 of this Book. One significant point here is that the numbers 22, 17, 110, and 55 are fixed integers—they cannot be changed at any time in the execution of the program. The dimensions for child windows may be altered during program execution.

The About dialog box style, DS_MODALFRAME | WS_CAPTION | WS_ SYSMENU, is discussed in Rector 3.1, p. 567. The caption (title bar) appears at the top of the dialog box. Style WS_SYSMENU is redundant for most dialog boxes that have a logic element (such as a pushbutton), since all that WS_SYSMENU adds is a dashbox at the top left of the box or an "X" at the top right of the box which may be picked by the user to exit the dialog box. The pushbutton serves the same immediate purpose in that it also destroys the dialog box. However, picking the pushbutton sends a message to the dialog box controlling procedure, AboutProc( ); picking the dashbox or "X" allows the user to destroy the dialog box without passing through the dialog box controlling procedure.

CTEXT in the template means "centered text," and PUSHBUTTON is a standard pushbutton (Petzold 3.1, pp. 420 & 431, and Rector 3.1, pp. 579-580 & Table 9.4, p. 585). Each of the four lines of print within the About box (after CAPTION) describes a dialog box control. The CTEXT entries are "static" controls, which means that the user cannot pick them with a mouse to highlight them and they do not accept keyboard input; the PUSHBUTTON is a predefined, non-static control. Each control has six elements:

For static controls (CTEXT, LTEXT, etc.):

- Text to be shown in the dialog box, in double quotes
- A control ID number, which is not called a handle in the windows texts, but performs the same function. It is a unique number assigned to a logic element. If the control is static the handle is never used, so it is assigned the number -1 by tradition. This is the same unique ID number that was discussed in Section 3 of this book.
- Four integers which specify the location of the top left corner of this control element with respect to the dialog box, and the control element width and height

For the non-static pushbutton control, these six elements are required:

- Text to be shown in the pushbutton center. In line 216 the text is OK.
- A control ID number. The seven possible predefined IDs are IDOK, IDYES, IDNO, IDCANCEL, IDABORT, IDIGNORE, and IDRETRY (Rector 3.1, p. 585). Other types of controls are assigned names like IDC_SCROLL1, which are defined as integers in a header file (like RESOURCE.H or MAINMAIN.H). These seven predefined ID numbers may be used in *any* control (not just pushbuttons).

  In the case of the pushbutton the ID is sent as a "wParam" value to the procedure controlling the window in which the pushbutton resides when the pushbutton is picked with the mouse (or in some cases, when a particular keyboard key is depressed).
- Four integers which specify the location of the top left corner of this control element with respect to the dialog box, and the control element width and height

The statement that ties all elements of the window together and initiates all action is DialogBox( ), line 412. DialogBox( ) has four arguments:

- hInst, the instance running at this time
- AboutBox, the symbolic name of the dialog box template in file MAINMAIN.RC, line 210
- ghWnd, the handle to the window that owns the dialog box
- lpProcAbout, the handle to the AboutProc( ) procedure. This handle was assigned to procedure AboutProc( ) in line 411, and it is invoked in line 412 because DialogBox( ) is responsible for creating an entirely new set of executable code within the compiler that will represent the dialog box in the final compiled version of MAINMAIN.

Note that "lpProcAbout" is a handle to a BOOLEAN procedure; it is not a handle to the final version of the window procedure that the compiler will create. The compiler assigns an internal handle name to the created modal dialog box window procedure; that handle name is not revealed (and is of no interest) because the dialog box must be attended to by the user immediately and destroyed by an EndDialog( ) statement. Modal dialog box creation, use, and destruction is all a "closed" sequence. If the developer wants further access to a dialog box it must be created as a modeless dialog box. In the modeless dialog box case the developer assigns a handle name to its window before the CreateDialog( ) statement and is able to access the dialog box freely.

DialogBox( ) calls the CreateWindowEx( ) function implicitly to create the dialog box. CreateWindowEx( ) issues a WM_INITDIALOG message to the AboutProc( ) procedure which controls the dialog box. The message is trapped at line 503. Line 504 returns TRUE so the input focus to this dialog box will be automatically set to the pushbutton, which is the first active logic element.

QUESTION: What does it mean to "set the input focus" to a logic element?

ANSWER: In visual terms, it means the logic element will be "highlighted." For example, if the element is a pushbutton, that pushbutton is darkened around the edges to display it more prominently.

The more important use of setting the focus occurs when keyboard input is received from the user and "focused" to a particular logic element.

Two events may occur:

- The user begins typing immediately, so the focus must have been set earlier by the program to the correct logic element to receive the input (else the input goes nowhere).

- The user picks a logic element with the mouse (highlighting it), then types the input. In this case the default "focus" set by the program has been overridden by the user.

In either case the setting of a default focus by the program for keyboard input is extremely important.

At this point DialogBox( ), line 412, has not relinquished control of the program. As soon as the user picks the dialog pushbutton or depresses the Enter key, a WM_COMMAND message is issued. If the user picks the **OK** pushbutton in the dialog box then wParam is set to IDOK; if the user depresses the Enter key wParam is set to IDCANCEL.

The WM_COMMAND message is trapped by line 505. Line 506 executes, then line 507, which begins to close the dialog box. As soon as the dialog box closes, DialogBox( ), line 412, yields control, and line 413 frees the dialog box procedure instance completely (which means that the stack allocated to the dialog box is freed for later use by another element).

The main window returns to its original state.

Start MainMain Construct and Sequencing The only active element remaining in this project is the second menu item, Start MainMain. Recall that at main window creation WM_SIZE and WM_CREATE message were sent to WndProc( ) to provide for computation of global variables StartX and StartY, and creation of a large font with a handle name "ghFont." Once that menu item is picked by the user, line 207 in MAINMAIN.RC initiates a WM_COMMAND message with wParam set to IDM_STARTSWITCH. The message is trapped in WndProc( ) at line 409 and again at line 416.

- START is set to TRUE so the screen will be painted later in line 441 (in the WM_PAINT case). The main window was immediately painted at creation but a default paint command, lines 444-445, was used to paint the blank screen.

- Line 418, the InvalidateRect( ) statement, commands the system to repaint the main window immediately, and this time START = TRUE.

TIP: Do not be overly concerned with the details of placing text on the main window. Concentrate on the ability to fix or float the initial main window presentation. Book 3, *Painting the Screen*, will discuss screen painting.

- Line 419, the break statement, returns control to the main window loop, lines 350-352.

- Since the InvalidateRect( ) statement has commanded repaint, a WM_ PAINT message is issued by the windows system to procedure WndProc( ). The message is trapped at line 428.

- Since START = TRUE, the main window is painted (lines 429-440). Then START is reset to FALSE, so nothing further happens until the menu item Start MainMain is again picked by the user.

This ends all discussion on how MAINMAIN works.

Exercising MAINMAIN Load the MAINMAIN project into the VWB according to the New Project Loading Sequence found at the front of the book. These kinds of tests should be performed by the developer:

- Recompile and rerun MAINMAIN using three different statements in the AboutBox template, line 211:

  - **STYLE DS_MODALFRAME | WS_CAPTION | WS_SYSMENU**
    This style produces an AboutBox with a caption "About MainMain" and a dashbox at the top left corner or an "X" at the top right corner of the dialog box. When the dashbox is picked the user is offered a Move capability or a Close capability (Windows 3.1). If Windows 95, picking the "X" closes the window immediately. The window close function has already been built into the pushbutton however, so the entire WM_SYSMENU system is redundant.

  - **STYLE DS_MODALFRAME | WS_CAPTION** This style eliminates the dashbox or "X" (System menu) from the dialog box.

  - **STYLE DS_MODALFRAME | WS_SYSMENU** This style produces the same result as "DS_MODALFRAME | WS_CAPTION | WS_SYSMENU." This is an oddity of all overlapped windows (formal and popup dialog boxes); the WS_SYSMENU style should not function properly without explicitly invoking the WS_CAPTION style, but it does. However, the writer recommends that WS_CAPTION always be entered explicitly when WS_SYSMENU is required.

  Similar tests will be performed below with the main window creation statement, using line 342.

- Recompile MAINMAIN using either the style in line 324 or line 325. To show the difference between the two styles, *always reset the size of the main window after each cycle.* That is, pick **Start MainMain**, observe the result, change the window size by capturing the lower-right corner of the main window with the mouse and dragging it to another location, and recycle Start MainMain again. The developer will find that a class "NULL" causes the program to overwrite the text indiscriminately, whereas "CS_VREDRAW | CS_HREDRAW" clears the screen display after each size change.

- Recompile MAINMAIN using either style above, but invoke only one of the CreateWindow( ) statements (lines 342, 343, or 344). What this shows is that the initial window position may be fixed by the developer or left to float. It also shows that "mixed" settings, such as line 344, do not work.

- Operate MAINMAIN with either the standard ShowWindow( ) statement in line 346, or the form that maximizes the window initially, line 348. If line 348 is used, the window creation statement (line 342) should probably be used (the form that uses default dimensions CW_ USEDEFAULT) because these dimensions are superfluous if the window is to be maximized initially.

- Try different main window frames. The window style used in line 342 is WS_OVERLAPPEDWINDOW, which is defined in include file WINDOWS.H as WS_OVERLAPPED | WS_CAPTION | WS_ SYSMENU | WS_THICKFRAME | WS_MINIMIZEBOX | WS_ MAXIMIZEBOX. If the developer desires to try different window frames around the main window, replace the "WS_OVER-LAPPEDWINDOW" in line 342 with (for example):

  - WS_OVERLAPPED | WS_CAPTION | WS_SYSMENU| WS_ DLGFRAME | WS_MINIMIZEBOX | WS_MAXIMIZEBOX

  - WS_OVERLAPPED | WS_CAPTION | WS_SYSMENU | WS_ BORDER | WS_MINIMIZEBOX | WS_MAXIMIZEBOX

  However, the WS_THICKFRAME always seems to look the best, and it is the *only* frame that allows the user to resize the window with the mouse by dragging the lower-right corner of the window to a new position. The Visual C++ instructions on using these styles states that *if* WS_CAPTION is included, then WS_DLGFRAME or WS_BORDER should *not* be included, and adherence to this rule is recommended. [See Rector 3.1, p. 137.]

- Verify the contributions of styles WS_CAPTION, WS_SYSMENU, WS_THICKFRAME, WS_MINIMIZEBOX, and WS_MAXIMIZEBOX. For these tests style WS_OVERLAPPEDWINDOW in line 342 has been disabled and replaced with its full definition:
  WS_OVERLAPPED | WS_CAPTION | WS_SYSMENU |
  WS_THICKFRAME | WS_MINIMIZEBOX| WS_MAXIMIZEBOX

  - **Test 1** Disable styles WS_MINIMIZEBOX and WS_MAXI-MIZEBOX in line 342, recompile, and rerun. Confirm that the minimize and maximize boxes at the top right of the main window disappear.

  - **Test 2** Disable style WS_SYSMENU in line 342 (but keep style WS_CAPTION). Recompile and rerun MAINMAIN. Note that the title bar is present but not the dashbox or "X" (System menu). Since the dashbox is the only means of terminating the main window, this is a bad option (eliminating the WS_SYSMENU style). Reboot the computer to terminate the program, re-enter the VWB, and restore WS_SYSMENU to line 342.

Note that the presence or absence of style WS_SYSMENU in the main window creation statement has no effect on the main window menu bar, Begin.

- **Test 3**   Disable style WS_THICKFRAME in 342. Recompile and rerun MAINMAIN. Confirm that the user is unable to pick and drag the lower-right corner of the main window to change its size.

- **Test 4**   This test does not work as advertised, but it is shown just in case the developer is curious. When style WS_CAPTION is disabled in line 342 the main window should be unable to display a title bar and System menu dashbox, but it does so anyway. For this test restore WS_THICKFRAME, WS_MINIMIZEBOX, and WS_MAXI-MIZEBOX in line 342 (only WS_CAPTION need be disabled). Confirm that the window creation works just as well without the WS_CAPTION style. However, do not play games in code development; keep the WS_CAPTION style in the creation statement anyway.

If a main window may be maximized initially and need never be decreased in size (such as a SETUP program, for example), then an acceptable style would be WS_OVERLAPPED | WS_CAPTION | WS_SYSMENU. This produces a screen window that cannot be reduced in size. To make the screen full size, replace line 346 with 348. However, most programs with any substance must provide for minimizing the window (reducing to icon size) so the user can temporarily move it aside to attend to other applications on the main window.

- To try other fonts and text sizes, change lines 312 and 313. To change the length of the line underlining the text, change lines 433-434. To change the width of the line, change line 431.

MainMain Closure   When most developers begin programming in windows they are encouraged to move quickly past the main window boilerplate that describes how the main window is formed in Windows 3.X or 4.X. Now the developer knows why: There aren't any exciting options there! For example, there is one useful main window frame size (WS_THICKFRAME), one way to close the main window using the System menu (WM_SYSMENU), choices

on whether or not the window should be allowed to increase to full-screen size
or icon size after it is initially opened (WS_MINIMIZEBOX /
WS_MAXIMIZEBOX), choices on main window menu bar/no main window
menu bar [not a WS style], and title bar/no title bar (WS_CAPTION) options.

Book 1   Figure 4-3

```
Program MAINMAIN files:
  1.  *.DEF, module-definition file
  2.  *.H,   header file
  3.  *.RC,  resource script file
  4.  *.C,   WinMain( ), WndProc( ), AboutProc( )


/***************************************************************/

001: ; MAINMAIN.DEF module-definition file -- used by LINK.EXE
002: NAME    MainMain    ;  Application's module name
003: DESCRIPTION 'Displays Words "On With the Show !",Underlined'
004: EXETYPE  WINDOWS  ;   Required for all Windows applications

005: STUB   'WINSTUB.EXE'; Generates error message if application
                         ;  is run without Windows
006: ;CODE can be moved in memory and discarded/reloaded
007: CODE  PRELOAD MOVEABLE DISCARDABLE
008: ;DATA must be MULTIPLE if program invoked more than once
009: DATA  PRELOAD MOVEABLE MULTIPLE
010: HEAPSIZE    1024    ; STACKSIZE no longer entered in *.DEF


/***************************************************************/

101: /* MAINMAIN.H (header file) */
102: #define IDM_ABOUT        10
103: #define IDM_STARTSWITCH  15


/***************************************************************/

201: /* MAINMAIN.RC (resource script file) */
202: #include <windows.h>
203: #include "mainmain.h"

204: MainMainMenu MENU
205:   {POPUP        "&Begin"
206:     {MENUITEM "&About MainMain...", IDM_ABOUT
207:     MENUITEM  "&Start MainMain ",   IDM_STARTSWITCH
208:     }
209:   }
```

```
210: AboutBox DIALOG 22, 17, 110, 55
211: STYLE DS_MODALFRAME | WS_CAPTION | WS_SYSMENU
212: CAPTION "About MainMain"
213:   {CTEXT "MainMain Application"        -1,  0,  5, 110,  8
214:   CTEXT "Microsoft Windows 3.1 and 4.0" -1,  0, 15, 110,  8
215:   CTEXT "Copyright \251 R. Braden, 1994" -1,  0, 25, 110,  8
216:   PUSHBUTTON "OK"                  IDOK, 39, 36,  32, 14
217:   }
```

/**/

```
301: /*  MAINMAIN.C, R. Braden */
302: #define STRICT
303: #include <windows.h>
304: #include <stdio.h; /* For "sprintf" */
305: #include "mainmain.h"

306: long FAR PASCAL _export WndProc(HWND, UINT, WPARAM, LPARAM);
307: BOOL FAR PASCAL _export AboutProc(HWND, UINT,WPARAM,LPARAM);

308: HANDLE hInst;
309: HWND   ghWnd;
310: RECT   rect1;

311: HFONT ghFont;  /* Font size and type */
312: PSTR pszFace = "MsSerif";
313: int iPtSize = 24; /* 24 point text; 72 points = 1 inch */

314: BOOL START = FALSE;
315: int StartX, StartY;
316: char szTemp[80]; /* For MessageBox( ) */

317: int PASCAL
     WinMain(HINSTANCE hInstance,HINSTANCE hPrevInstance,
       LPSTR lpCmdLine, int nCmdShow)
318:   {MSG msg;
319:   WNDCLASS wc;
320:   ATOM aWndClass;

321:   if(!hPrevInstance)
322:     {/* Main window */
323: /* Alternative styles "NULL" and "CS_VREDRAW|CS_HREDRAW" */
       /* Enable one of the two for any given run */
324:     wc.style = NULL;
325:     /* wc.style = CS_VREDRAW | CS_HREDRAW; */

326:     wc.lpfnWndProc = WndProc;
```

```
327:    wc.cbClsExtra = 0;
328:    wc.cbWndExtra = 0;
329:    wc.hInstance = hInstance;
330:    wc.hIcon = LoadIcon(NULL, IDI_APPLICATION);
331:    wc.hCursor = LoadCursor(NULL, IDC_ARROW);
332:    wc.hbrBackground = GetStockObject(WHITE_BRUSH);
333:    wc.lpszMenuName =  "MainMainMenu";
334:    wc.lpszClassName = "MainMainWClass";

335:    aWndClass = RegisterClass(&wc);
336:    if(!aWndClass) MessageBox(NULL,
337:      "Failure to register Main Window Class.",NULL,MB_OK);
338:      }

339:    /* Save instance handle in a static (global) variable,  */
        /* to be used in subsequent window calls.              */
340:    hInst = hInstance;

341:    /* Enable only 1 of these 3 CreateWindow( ) statements  at
        a time */

342:  ghWnd=CreateWindow("MainMainwClass","MainMain Application",
          WS_OVERLAPPED| WS_SYSMENU | WS_MINIMIZEBOX|
          WS_MAXIMIZEBOX | WS_THICKFRAME
          /* WS_OVERLAPPEDWINDOW */, CW_USEDEFAULT, CW_USEDEFAULT,
          CW_USEDEFAULT, CW_USEDEFAULT, NULL, NULL, hInst, NULL);

343:/*ghWnd=CreateWindow("MainMainWClass","MainMain Application",
       WS_OVERLAPPEDWINDOW,1,60,600,400,NULL,NULL,hInst,NULL);*/

344:/*ghWnd=CreateWindow("MainMainWClass","MainMain Application",
          WS_OVERLAPPEDWINDOW, 1, CW_USEDEFAULT,600,400,NULL,NULL,
          hInst,NULL); */

345:   /* Make window visible; update its client area */
346:   ShowWindow(ghWnd, nCmdShow);
347:   /* Alternate ShowWindow( ) maximizes main window size */
348:   /* ShowWindow(ghWnd, SW_SHOWMAXIMIZED); */
349:   UpdateWindow(ghWnd);

350:   while(GetMessage(&msg, NULL, NULL, NULL))
351:     {TranslateMessage(&msg) ;
352:     DispatchMessage(&msg) ;
353:     }

354:   return(msg.wParam);
355:   } /* End of WinMain( )  */
```

```
/**************************************************************/

401: long FAR PASCAL _export
     WndProc(HWND haWnd,UINT msg,WPARAM wParam,LPARAM lParam)
402: {DLGPROC lpProcAbout;/* Pointer to "AboutProc" function*/
403: HDC       hdc;
404: PAINTSTRUCT ps;
405: POINT      pt;
406: HPEN    lhPen,lhOldPen;

408: switch(msg)
409:    {case WM_COMMAND:
410:      if(wParam == IDM_ABOUT)
411:        {lpProcAbout=(DLGPROC)MakeProcInstance((FARPROC)
            AboutProc, hInst);
412:        DialogBox(hInst, "AboutBox", haWnd, lpProcAbout);
413:        FreeProcInstance((FARPROC)lpProcAbout);
414:        break;
415:        }
416:      else if(wParam == IDM_STARTSWITCH)
417:        {START = TRUE;
418:        InvalidateRect(haWnd, &rect1, FALSE);
419:        break;
420:        }
421:      else /* Let Windows process message */
422:        return(DefWindowProc(haWnd, msg, wParam, lParam));

423:    case WM_CREATE:
424:      /* Create font of size "iPtSize" with type "pszFace"*/
425:      ghFont = CreateFont(-iPtSize,0,0,0,FW_HEAVY,0,0,0,0,0,
            0,0,0, pszFace);
427:      break;

428:    case WM_PAINT:
429:      if(START)
430:        {hdc = BeginPaint(haWnd, &ps);
431:         lhPen = CreatePen(PS_SOLID, 4, RGB(0,0,0));
432:         lhOldPen = SelectObject(hdc, lhPen);;
433:         MoveToEx(hdc, StartX - 125, StartY + 20, &pt);
434:         LineTo(hdc, StartX + 125, StartY + 20);
435:         SelectObject(hd,lhOldPen);
436:         DeleteObject(lhPen);
437:         SelectObject(hdc, ghFont);
438:         SetTextAlign(hdc, TA_CENTER);
439:         TextOut(hdc, StartX, StartY - 20,
              "On With the Show !", 18);
```

```
440:        EndPaint(haWnd, &ps);
441:        START = FALSE;
442:        }
443:     else
444:        {hdc = BeginPaint(haWnd, &ps);
445:        EndPaint(haWnd, &ps);
446:        }

446A:      /* MessageBox(ghWnd,"Just Painted Main Window",
              "PAINT MESSAGE",MB_OK); */

447:     break;

448:     case WM_SIZE:
449:        GetClientRect(haWnd, &rect1);
450:        /* Calculate the middle of the client area */
451:        StartX = (rect1.right - rect1.left) / 2;
452:        StartY = (rect1.bottom - rect1.top) / 2;

452A:      /* sprintf(szTemp,"Center X & Y Coordinates: %d   %d",
              StartX, StartY);
452B:        MessageBox(ghWnd,szTemp,"WM_SIZE MESSAGE",MB_OK); */

453:        break;

454:     case WM_DESTROY: /* Message: window being destroyed */
455:        PostQuitMessage(0);
456:        break;

457:     default:  /* Passes message on if unproccessed */
458:        return(DefWindowProc(haWnd, msg, wParam, lParam));
459:        }
460:    return NULL;
461:    } /* End of WndProc( ) */

/***************************************************************/

501: BOOL FAR PASCAL _export
     AboutProc(HWND hDlg, UINT msg, WPARAM wParam, LPARAM lParam)
502:    {switch(msg)
503:     {case WM_INITDIALOG:
504:        return TRUE;
505:     case WM_COMMAND:
506:        if(wParam == IDOK || wParam == IDCANCEL)
507:          {EndDialog(hDlg, TRUE);
508:          return TRUE;
509:          }
```

```
510:       break;
511:     }
512:   return FALSE;
513:   } /* End of AboutProc( ) */

/**************************************************************/
```

Figure 4-3:   File listing of project MainMain

Section 5

Projects PAYUP

This program demonstrates the use of modal dialog boxes to present data to and receive data from a user. It also makes frequent use of message boxes to inform the user when an apparent error has occurred.

LOGIC DIAGRAMS

The logic diagrams for the non-windowed and windowed versions of PAYUP are the same. Both programs perform the same internal computations; the only difference is the method used to interface with the user.

Non-Windowed Version of PAYUP A logic diagram of the non-windowed version of PAYUP is shown in Figure 5-1, Part One. The source code and executable code for this version are located in subdirectory PAYUPNW. The source code listing for the program is shown in Figure 5-2, for reference only.

Windowed Versions of PAYUP A logic diagram of the windowed versions of PAYUP is shown in Figure 5-1, Part Two. The source code listing for the initial program is shown in Figure 5-3. Four files are necessary to fully describe the windowed version of project PAYUP (*.DEF, *.H, *.RC, and *.C). The files shown in Figure 5-3 have unique line numbers assigned so they may be discussed in detail in the sections that follow.

Project PAYUP Logic Sequence (Non-Windowed and Windowed Versions) These are shown in Figure 5-1, Parts One and Two.

- Project PAYUP asks the user to enter a starting loan amount and an annual interest rate. As soon as the interest rate is entered, PAYUP checks that the interest rate is between 5.0 and 25.0 to ensure that the user does not

79

enter an incorrect number such as ".08" to mean an eight percent interest rate. If the interest rate number entered is not between 5.0 and 25.0, the program displays an error message and recycles to ask the user for a new interest rate.

- Next, the program computes a minimum monthly payment which is 1/12th of the annual interest due on the initial loan value. This minimum monthly payment is displayed for the user when she/he chooses a monthly payment.

- The user is asked to enter a monthly payment. If the monthly payment is less than the computed minimum monthly payment, an error message is displayed and the user is asked to re-enter the monthly payment.

- The three entries (initial loan amount, annual interest rate, and monthly payment) are displayed for the user, and the user is asked if the numbers are correct. If correct, the program continues. If not, the program recycles to ask for new input data.

- The computation is made on how many months it takes to pay off the loan. This number is displayed to the user.

- The user is asked if the program should be rerun. If the user answers Yes, he/she is immediately asked if the same starting loan amount and interest rate should be used. If the answer is Yes, the only new input data is the monthly payment. If the user answers No the program recycles to the top of the program to receive all new inputs.

- If the user answers No to the first question above (Rerun the Program ?), the user is asked if an amortization table should be printed. If the answer is Yes, the table is printed; if No, no table is printed.

- The program quits.

WINDOWS PROJECT FILES LAYOUTS

The file layouts for the windowed versions of PAYUP are approximately the same as shown in project MAINMAIN for WinMain( ) and WndProc( ). However, an additional computational/windows procedure named CalcProc( ) has been added to control all the popup modal dialog boxes except the AboutBox, which is already controlled by procedure AboutProc( ).

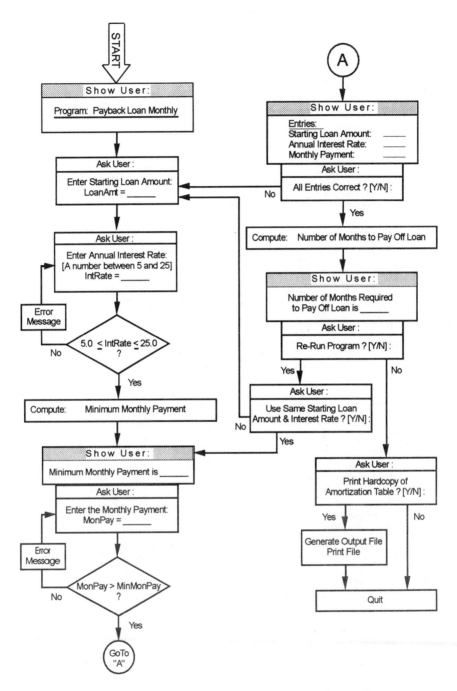

Figure 5-1 Part One: Program PAYUP.C logic, non-windowed version

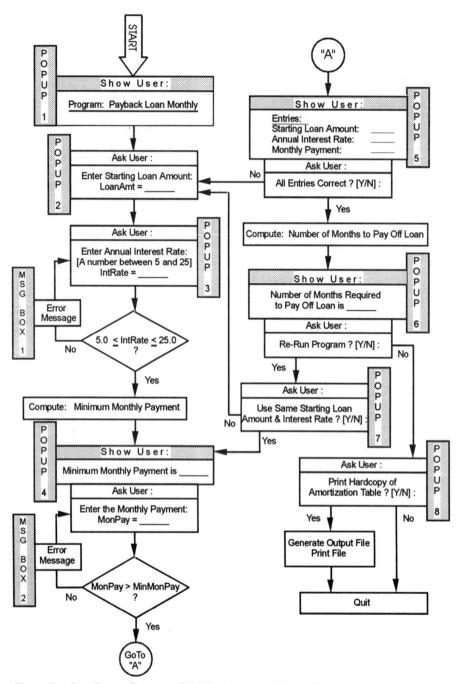

Figure 5-1 Part Two: Program PAYUP.C logic, windowed version

PAYUP VERSIONS

There are three versions of project PAYUP discussed and demonstrated. They are:

- **PAYUP1** This is the simplest version of PAYUP. It builds six empty modal dialog boxes that will be filled-in later. The developer is shown two methods for starting the program, both of which are used in commercial software applications:
  - Through the Begin main window menu
  - Through a technique that bypasses the main window menu and starts the program as soon as the main window is created. Unfortunately it bypasses the AboutBox also, so the developer who uses this technique must insert the AboutBox information at another place in the application, or leave it out.

- **PAYUP2** This version fills the six empty dialog boxes shown in PAYUP1 with controls that present data to and take data from the user. It adds a seventh dialog box which is necessary for recycling the program.

- **PAYUP3** This version enhances PAYUP2 with the code necessary to print an amortization table for the user once she/he has settled on the correct loan amount, interest rate, and monthly payment. The new code added to this project is taken from an existing Microsoft demonstration project named PRNTFILE.

Book 1   Figure 5-2

```
/*  Program "payup.c." User enters loan amount, interest rate, */
/*  and monthly payment. Program runs out monthly data. Dec 92 */

#include <stdio.h>
#include <stdlib.h>

main( )
  {float LOANAMT,INTRATE,PAYMENT,MINMONPAY,AMT,AINT,PAYDOWN;
  float FRACTION, BIGANSWER;
  char letter, loop, reply, answer, tellme, FILEOPEN;
  FILE *ptr; int KK;
```

```
   printf("\n\n\n\n\n");
   printf("\n\t\t\t PROGRAM:  PAYBACK LOAN MONTHLY ");
   printf("\n\t\t\t ---------------------------- \n");

REINPUT:
   printf("\n\n\n\n\t\t    ENTER STARTING LOAN AMOUNT : ");
   scanf("%f,"&LOANAMT); fflush(stdin);

   loop = 'Y'; while(loop == 'Y')
     {printf("\n\n\t\t\t  ENTER THE INTEREST RATE : \n");
     printf("\t\t    FOR EXAMPLE, IF THE RATE IS TEN PERCENT,\n");
     printf("\t\t\t\t ENTER '10.0'.   ");
     scanf("%f,"&INTRATE); fflush(stdin);
     if((INTRATE >= 5.0) && (INTRATE <= 25.0)) loop = 'N';
     }

   MINMONPAY = LOANAMT * INTRATE / 1200.;
   RIGHTHERE: loop = 'Y'; while(loop == 'Y')
     {printf("\n\n\t\t    MINIMUM MONTHLY PAYMENT IS $%7.2f .\n,"
       MINMONPAY);
     printf("\n\n\t\t      ENTER THE MONTHLY PAYMENT : ");
     scanf("%f,"&PAYMENT); fflush(stdin);
     if(PAYMENT <= MINMONPAY)
printf("\n\t\t ERROR:  MONTHLY PAYMENT TOO LOW.  TRY AGAIN .\n");
     else
       loop = 'N';
     }

   loop = 'Y'; while(loop == 'Y')
     {printf("\n\n\t\t\t   THE ENTRIES ARE :");
     printf("\n\t\t\t   -----------------------");
     printf("\n\t\t\t   LOAN AMOUNT: %10.2f "LOANAMT);
     printf("\n\t\t\t   INTEREST RATE:  %7.3f ,"INTRATE);
     printf("\n\t\t\t   MONTHLY PAYMENT: %7.2f \n,"PAYMENT);
     printf("\n\t\t\t ALL ENTRIES CORRECT ? [Y/N] : ");
     answer = toupper(getch( )); printf("\n");
     if((answer == 'Y') || (answer == 'N')) loop = 'N';
     }

   if(answer == 'N') goto REINPUT;
   KK = 0; AMT = LOANAMT;
   while(AMT >= 0.0)
     {KK++;
     AINT = AMT * INTRATE / 1200.0 ;
     PAYDOWN = PAYMENT - AINT;
```

```
   AMT = AMT - PAYMENT + AINT;
   }

FRACTION = AMT / PAYMENT;
BIGANSWER = KK + FRACTION;
printf("\n\t\t Number of Months to Pay Off Loan is %7.2f . \n,"
  BIGANSWER);

loop = 'Y'; while(loop == 'Y')
  {printf("\n\t\t\t  RE-RUN THE PROGRAM ? [Y/N] : ");
  answer = toupper(getch( )); printf("\n");
  if((answer == 'Y') || (answer == 'N')) loop = 'N';
  }

if(answer == 'Y')
  {loop = 'Y'; while(loop == 'Y')
    {printf(
"\n\t   USE SAME STARTING LOAN AMOUNT AND INTEREST RATE ? [Y/N] : ");
    tellme = toupper(getch( )); printf("\n");
    if((tellme == 'Y') || (tellme == 'N')) loop = 'N';
    }

  if(tellme == 'Y') goto RIGHTHERE;
  else goto REINPUT;
  }

/* All re-runs complete */
loop = 'Y'; while(loop == 'Y')
  {printf(
       "\n\t\t   PRINT A HARDCOPY OF THE RESULTS ? [Y/N] : ");
  reply = toupper(getch( )); printf("\n");
  if(( reply == 'Y') || (reply == 'N')) loop = 'N';
  }

if(reply == 'Y')
  {/* Open file 'TEMP.DOC' */
  if((ptr=fopen("TEMP.DOC,""w+")) == NULL)
    {printf(
        "\n\tCan't open file 'TEMP.DOC' to record output. \n");
    printf("\n\t\t\tPress any key to continue . . . \n");
    letter = getch( );
    FILEOPEN = 'N';
    }
  else FILEOPEN = 'Y';
  if(FILEOPEN == 'Y')
```

```
{KK = 0; AINT = 0.0; PAYDOWN = 0.0;
AMT = LOANAMT;
fprintf(ptr,"\t\t\t    LOAN AMOUNT:   %10.2f \n,"LOANAMT);
fprintf(ptr,"\t\t\t    INTEREST RATE:   %7.3f \n,"INTRATE);
fprintf(ptr,"\t\t\t   MONTHLY PAYMENT: %7.2f \n\n,"PAYMENT);
fprintf(ptr,
"\t\tNUM.   PAYMENT   INTEREST   PAYDOWN   NEW PRINCIPLE\n");
fprintf(ptr,
"\t\t---- --------- -------- --------- -------------\n");
fprintf(ptr,
     "\t\t%3d                                 %9.2f \n,"
  KK,AMT);

while(AMT >= 0.0)
  {KK++;
  AINT = AMT * INTRATE / 1200.0 ;
  PAYDOWN = PAYMENT - AINT;
  AMT = AMT - PAYMENT + AINT;
  fprintf(ptr,"\t\t%3d   %9.2f %9.2f   %9.2f    %9.2f \n,"
    KK, PAYMENT,AINT,PAYDOWN,AMT);
  }

fclose(ptr);
system("PRINT TEMP.DOC");
  }
}
} /* End of payup.c */
```

Figure 5-2:   Program PAYUP.C listing, non-windowed version

PAYUP1 SEQUENCE OF EVENTS

Load the PAYUP1 project into the VWB according to the New Project Loading Sequence found at the front of the book. Project PAYUP1 demonstrates how a series of popup modal dialog boxes is processed sequentially in a windows program. Since each dialog box is "modal," each must be attended to by the user before the program will continue. The "modeless" dialog box, the type that may be created on the screen and need *not* be attended to by the user, is shown in detail in Book 2, *Child Windows*. All references below are to Figure 5-3, PAYUP1 source listing, windowed version:

- Lines 001-011 are file PAYUP1.DEF, the module definition file.

- Lines 101-103 are the PAYUP1.H header file.
- Lines 201-255 are the PAYUP1.RC resource script file.
- Lines 301-693 are the PAYUP1.C source file.
  - All global definitions appear in lines 301-310, to include function prototypes, global handle names, and a global integer named nCOUNTER. nCOUNTER is used in WinMain( ), WndProc( ), and CalcProc( ) to indicate which dialog box is currently being processed.
  - WinMain( ) is shown as lines 311-342.
  - WndProc( ) is shown as lines 401-456.
  - AboutProc( ) is shown as lines 501-513.
  - CalcProc( ) is shown as lines 601-693.

WinMain( ) in PAYUP1 is identical to WinMain( ) in MAINMAIN except that:

- nCOUNTER is initialized in line 334.
- An alternative method of starting PAYUP1 initially is provided by line 336, which transfers program control directly to WndProc( ), message WM_COMMAND, wParam = IDM_CALC, bypassing the main window menu. It is provided so the developer can understand this alternative program start-up method.

The project's main message loop is in lines 337-340.

Book 1   Figure 5-3

```
Program PAYUP1 files:
  1.  *.DEF, module-definition file
  2.  *.H,   header file
  3.  *.RC,  resource script file
  4.  *.C,   WinMain( ), WndProc( ), AboutProc( ), CalcProc( )


/****************************************************************/

001: ; PAYUP1.DEF module-definition file -- used by LINK.EXE

002: ; ***********************************************
     ; *   This version of PAYUP uses:            *
     ; *     1.  Program entry via:               *
     ; *           *  "Begin" main menu, or       *
     ; *           *  "PostMessage" statement at end of  *
     ; *              program initialization.     *
     ; *     2.  Popup dialog box windows only.   *
     ; ***********************************************
```

```
003: NAME      Payup     ;  Application's module name
004: DESCRIPTION  'Computes Number of Months to Pay Off a Loan'
005: EXETYPE   WINDOWS  ;  Required for all  Windows applications
006: STUB   'WINSTUB.EXE';  Generates error message if application
                          ;  is run without Windows
007: ;CODE can be moved in memory and discarded/reloaded
008: CODE   PRELOAD MOVEABLE DISCARDABLE
009: ;DATA must be MULTIPLE if program invoked more than once
010: DATA   PRELOAD MOVEABLE MULTIPLE
011: HEAPSIZE     1024
```

```
/****************************************************************/
```

```
101: /* PAYUP1.H (header file) */
102: #define IDM_ABOUT 10
103: #define IDM_CALC  15
```

```
/****************************************************************/
```

```
201: /* PAYUP1.RC (resource script file) */
202: #include <windows.h>
203: #include "payup1.h"
```

```
204: PayupMenu MENU
205:   {POPUP       "&Begin"
206:     {MENUITEM "&About Payup...," IDM_ABOUT
207:     MENUITEM "&Start Payup Program...," IDM_CALC
208:     }
209:   }
```

```
210: AboutBox DIALOG 22, 17, 110, 55
211: STYLE DS_MODALFRAME | WS_CAPTION
212: CAPTION "About Payup"
213:   {CTEXT "Payup Application"          -1,  0,  5, 110,  8
214:   CTEXT "Microsoft Windows 3.1 and 4.0" -1,  0, 15, 110,  8
215:   CTEXT "Copyright \251 R. Braden, 1994" -1,  0, 25, 110,  8
216:   PUSHBUTTON "OK"                    IDOK, 39, 36,  32, 14
217:   }
```

```
218: CalcBox1  DIALOG 50, 20, 160, 60
219: STYLE WS_DLGFRAME | WS_POPUP
220: FONT 10, "Ms Sans Serif"
221:   {CTEXT "Popup #1"    -1, 0,  5, 160, 8
222:   PUSHBUTTON "OK"  IDOK, 64, 40, 32, 14
223:   }
```

```
224: CalcBox2  DIALOG 50, 28, 160, 60
225: STYLE WS_DLGFRAME | WS_POPUP
226: FONT 10, "Ms Sans Serif"
227:   {CTEXT "Popup #2" -1, 0, 5, 160, 8
228:   PUSHBUTTON "OK" IDOK, 64, 40, 32, 14
229:   }

230: CalcBox3  DIALOG 50, 36, 160, 60
231: STYLE WS_DLGFRAME | WS_POPUP
232: FONT 10, "Ms Sans Serif"
233:   {CTEXT "Popup #3" -1, 0, 5, 160, 8
234:   PUSHBUTTON "OK" IDOK, 64, 40, 32, 14
235:   }

236: CalcBox4  DIALOG 50, 44, 160, 60
237: STYLE WS_DLGFRAME | WS_POPUP
238: FONT 10, "Ms Sans Serif"
239:   {CTEXT "Popup #4" -1, 0, 5, 160, 8
240:   PUSHBUTTON "OK" IDOK, 64, 40, 32, 14
241:   }

242: CalcBox5  DIALOG 50, 52, 160, 60
243: STYLE WS_DLGFRAME | WS_POPUP
244: FONT 10, "Ms Sans Serif"
245:   {CTEXT "Popup #5" -1, 0, 5, 160, 8
246:   PUSHBUTTON "OK" IDOK, 64, 40, 32, 14
247:   }

248: CalcBox6  DIALOG 50, 60, 160, 60
249: STYLE WS_DLGFRAME | WS_POPUP
250: FONT 10, "Ms Sans Serif"
251:   {CTEXT "Popup #6"        -1, 0, 5, 160, 8
252:   CTEXT "Re-Run Program ?" -1, 0, 20, 160, 8
253:   PUSHBUTTON "YES"     IDYES, 29, 40, 32, 14
254:   PUSHBUTTON "NO"      IDNO , 99, 40, 32, 14
255:   }

/****************************************************************/

301: /*  PAYUP1.C, R. Braden */
302: #define STRICT
303: #include <windows.h>
304: #include "payup1.h"

305: long FAR PASCAL _export WndProc(HWND, UINT, WPARAM, LPARAM);
306: BOOL FAR PASCAL _export AboutProc(HWND, UINT,WPARAM,LPARAM);
307: BOOL FAR PASCAL _export CalcProc(HWND, UINT, WPARAM,LPARAM);
```

```
308: HANDLE  hInst;
309: HWND    ghWnd;
310: int  nCOUNTER;

311: int PASCAL
     WinMain(HINSTANCE hInstance,HINSTANCE hPrevInstance,
     LPSTR lpCmdLine, int nCmdShow)
312: {MSG msg;
313: WNDCLASS wc;

314:   if(!hPrevInstance)
315:     {/* Main window */
316:     wc.style = NULL;
317:     wc.lpfnWndProc = WndProc;
318:     wc.cbClsExtra = 0;
319:     wc.cbWndExtra = 0;
320:     wc.hInstance = hInstance;
321:     wc.hIcon = LoadIcon(NULL, IDI_APPLICATION);
322:     wc.hCursor = LoadCursor(NULL, IDC_ARROW);
323:     wc.hbrBackground = GetStockObject(WHITE_BRUSH);
324:     wc.lpszMenuName =  "PayupMenu";
325:     wc.lpszClassName = "PayupWClass";
326:     RegisterClass(&wc);
327:     }

328:   /* Save the instance handle in a static (global)  */
       /* variable to be used in subsequent window calls. */
329:   hInst = hInstance;

330:  ghWnd=CreateWindow("PayupWClass,""Payup Application,"
        WS_OVERLAPPEDWINDOW, CW_USEDEFAULT,  CW_USEDEFAULT,
     CW_USEDEFAULT,CW_USEDEFAULT,NULL,NULL,hInstance,NULL);

331:   /* Make window visible; update its client area */
332:   ShowWindow(ghWnd, nCmdShow);
333:   UpdateWindow(ghWnd);

334:   nCOUNTER = 1; /* Start the program sequence */

335:   /* Enabling the next statement causes the  program to
        bypass the "Begin" main menu,  and  proceed directly
        into the PAYUP program. */
336:   /* PostMessage(ghWnd, WM_COMMAND, IDM_CALC, 0L); */
337:   while(GetMessage(&msg, NULL, NULL, NULL))
338:     {TranslateMessage(&msg);
339:     DispatchMessage(&msg);
```

```
340:    }

341:    return(msg.wParam);
342:    } /* End of WinMain( ) */

/****************************************************************/

401: long FAR PASCAL _export
     WndProc(HWND haWnd,UINT msg,WPARAM wParam,LPARAM lParam)
402:    {DLGPROC lpprocAbout;/* Pointer to "AboutProc" function */
403:    DLGPROC lpprocCalc;  /* Pointer to "CalcProc"  function */

404:  switch(msg)
405:    {case WM_COMMAND:
406:      if(wParam == IDM_ABOUT)
407:        {lpprocAbout=(DLGPROC)MakeProcInstance((FARPROC)
              AboutProc, hInst);
408:        DialogBox(hInst, "AboutBox," haWnd, lpprocAbout);
409:        FreeProcInstance((FARPROC)lpprocAbout);
410:        break;
411:        }

412:      else if(wParam == IDM_CALC)
413:        {switch(nCOUNTER)
414:          {case 1:
415:            lpprocCalc=(DLGPROC)MakeProcInstance((FARPROC)
                CalcProc, hInst);
416:            DialogBox(hInst, "CalcBox1," haWnd, lpprocCalc);
417:            FreeProcInstance((FARPROC)lpprocCalc);
418:            break;
419:          case 2:
420:            lpprocCalc=(DLGPROC)MakeProcInstance((FARPROC)
                CalcProc, hInst);
421:            DialogBox(hInst, "CalcBox2," haWnd, lpprocCalc);
422:            FreeProcInstance((FARPROC)lpprocCalc);
423:            break;
424:          case 3:
425:            lpprocCalc=(DLGPROC)MakeProcInstance((FARPROC)
                CalcProc, hInst);
426:            DialogBox(hInst, "CalcBox3," haWnd, lpprocCalc);
427:            FreeProcInstance((FARPROC)lpprocCalc);
428:            break;
429:          case 4:
430:            lpprocCalc=(DLGPROC)MakeProcInstance((FARPROC)
                CalcProc, hInst);
431:            DialogBox(hInst, "CalcBox4," haWnd, lpprocCalc);
432:            FreeProcInstance((FARPROC)lpprocCalc);
```

```
433:            break;
434:          case 5:
435:            lpprocCalc=(DLGPROC)MakeProcInstance((FARPROC)
                  CalcProc, hInst);
436:            DialogBox(hInst, "CalcBox5," haWnd, lpprocCalc);
437:            FreeProcInstance((FARPROC)lpprocCalc);
438:            break;
439:          case 6:
440:            lpprocCalc=(DLGPROC)MakeProcInstance((FARPROC)
                  CalcProc, hInst);
441:            DialogBox(hInst, "CalcBox6," haWnd, lpprocCalc);
442:            FreeProcInstance((FARPROC)lpprocCalc);
443:            break;
444:          }
445:        break;
446:        }

447:      else /* Let Windows process message */
448:        return(DefWindowProc(haWnd, msg, wParam, lParam));

449:    case WM_DESTROY: /* message: window being destroyed */
450:        PostQuitMessage(0);
451:        break;

452:    default:  /* Passes message on if unproccessed */
453:        return(DefWindowProc(haWnd, msg, wParam, lParam));
454:      }
455:   return NULL;
456: } /* End of WndProc( ) */

/***************************************************************/

501: BOOL FAR PASCAL _export
     AboutProc(HWND haDlg,UINT msg,WPARAM wParam,LPARAM lParam)
502: {switch(msg)
503:   {case WM_INITDIALOG:
504:      return TRUE;

505:    case WM_COMMAND:
506:      if(wParam == IDOK || wParam == IDCANCEL)
507:        {EndDialog(haDlg, TRUE);
508:        return TRUE;
509:        }
510:      break;
511:    }
512:   return FALSE;
513: } /* End of AboutProc( ) */
```

```
/****************************************************************/

601: BOOL FAR PASCAL _export
     CalcProc(HWND haDlg, UINT msg, WPARAM wParam, LPARAM lParam)
602:   {switch(msg)
603:     {case WM_INITDIALOG:
604:       switch(nCOUNTER)
605:         {case 1:  /* This program calculates . . . */
606:           return TRUE; /* Set input focus to pushbutton */
607:         case 2:  /* Enter the loan amount . . . */
608:           /* Set input focus to pushbutton for now */
609:           return TRUE;
610:         case 3:  /* Enter the interest rate . . . */
611:           /* Same as case 2 above */
612:           return TRUE;
613:         case 4:  /* Enter the monthly payment . . . */
614:           /* In later versions of this program a number(min-
              imum monthly payment) will be posted to the case 4
              popup window here,  using fcn SetDlgItemText( ) */
615:           return TRUE;
616:         case 5:  /* The entries are . . . */
617:           /* In later  versions  of this program,  3 numbers
              will be  posted to  the case 5 popup  window here,
              using function SetDlgItemText( ) */
618:           return TRUE;
619:         case 6:  /* The number of months to pay loan is . */
620:           /* In later  versions of  this program  the answer
              will be  posted to the  case 6 popup  window here,
              using function SetDlgTextItem( ) */
621:           return TRUE;
622:         } /* End of switch(nCOUNTER) */
623:       break;

624:     case WM_COMMAND:
625:       switch(nCOUNTER)
626:         {case 1:  /* This program calculates . . . */
627:           if(wParam == IDOK || wParam == IDCANCEL)
628:             {EndDialog(haDlg, TRUE);
629:             /* Set up the next popup window */
630:             nCOUNTER = 2;
631:             PostMessage(ghWnd, WM_COMMAND, IDM_CALC, OL);
632:             return TRUE;
633:             }
634:           break ;

635:         case 2:  /* Enter the loan amount . . . */
```

```
636:        if(wParam == IDOK || wParam == IDCANCEL)
637:        {/* In later versions of this program, the fcn
            GetDlgItemText( ) will be used here to get the
            loan amount off the popup window before it
            disappears */
638:        EndDialog(haDlg, TRUE);
639:        /* Set up the next popup window */
640:        nCOUNTER = 3;
641:        PostMessage(ghWnd, WM_COMMAND, IDM_CALC, OL);
642:        return TRUE;
643:        }
644:     break;

645:     case 3: /* Enter the interest rate . . . */
646:        if(wParam == IDOK || wParam == IDCANCEL)
647:        {/* In later versions of this program, the fcn
            GetDlgItemText( ) will be used here to get the
            interest rate off the popup window before it
            disappears */
648:        EndDialog(haDlg, TRUE);
649:        /* In later versions of this program a computa-
            tion will be made here to determine the minimum
            monthly payment because that number must be
            displayed on the next popup window */
650:        /* Set up the next popup window */
651:        nCOUNTER = 4;
652:        PostMessage(ghWnd, WM_COMMAND, IDM_CALC, OL);
653:        return TRUE;
654:        }
655:     break;

656:     case 4: /* Enter the monthly payment . . . */
657:        if(wParam == IDOK || wParam == IDCANCEL)
658:        {/* In later versions of this program, the fcn
            GetDlgItemText( ) will be used here to get the
            monthly payment off the popup window before it
            disappears */
659:        EndDialog(haDlg, TRUE);
660:        /* In later versions of this program a computa-
            tion will be made here to determine the number
            of months before the loan pays off. The answer
            is then posted to the case 5 popup window using
            SetDlgItemText( ) in the WM_INITDIALOG section*/
661:        /* Set up the next popup window */
662:        nCOUNTER = 5;
663:        PostMessage(ghWnd, WM_COMMAND, IDM_CALC, OL);
664:        return TRUE;
```

```
665:            }
666:            break;

667:        case 5: /* Show all entries . . . */
668:            if(wParam == IDOK || wParam == IDCANCEL)
669:              {EndDialog(haDlg, TRUE);
670:              /* Set up the next popup window */
671:              nCOUNTER = 6;
672:              PostMessage(ghWnd, WM_COMMAND, IDM_CALC, OL);
673:              return TRUE;
674:              }
675:            break;

676:        case 6:  /* Final answer is displayed here. */
677:            /* Rerun program ? */
678:            nCOUNTER = 1;
679:            if(wParam == IDYES)
680:              {PostMessage(ghWnd, WM_COMMAND, IDM_CALC, OL);
681:              EndDialog(haDlg, TRUE);
682:              return TRUE;
683:              }
684:            else if(wParam == IDNO || wParam == IDCANCEL)
685:              {EndDialog(haDlg, TRUE);
686:              return TRUE;
687:              }
688:            break;

689:          } /* End of switch(nCOUNTER) */
690:        break;
691:      } /* End of switch(msg) */
692:    return FALSE;
693:  } /* End of CalcProc( ) */

/****************************************************************/
```

Figure 5-3: Project PAYUP1 listing, windowed version

AboutBox, Dialog Box, and Message Box Constructs The general construction of these types of boxes is outlined below.

AboutBox The AboutBox in PAYUP1 is identical to the AboutBox in MAINMAIN. It is accessed by picking **Begin|About Payup...** at the main window, and presents the same AboutBox with copyright information, etc.

Dialog Boxes   These are all overlapped-style popup windows. According to Rector 3.1, p. 567, "A dialog box must be an overlapped window. It cannot have the WS_CHILD window style. Windows disables all child windows when their parent windows are disabled. A WS_CHILD style modal dialog box would disable its parent, which in turn would disable the child. Then because neither the parent nor the child can receive inputs, the dialog box would never terminate."

A child window cannot be a dialog box and its contents cannot be described in the *.RC template file. Yet every dialog box is filled with "child window controls," which have all the characteristics of child windows (they *are* child windows). One way to eliminate the quirks in nomenclature is to think of child window controls as "logic elements" and forget that they are a special form of child window.

No window can be created until the CreateWindow( ) or CreateWindowEx( ) statement has been executed. In the main window creation, CreateWindow( ) appears explicitly (line 330). For popup windows in PAYUP, the CreateWindow( ) statement is embedded in the DialogBox( ) statement, (e.g., line 416).

The main window is registered (line 326), created (line 330), then made visible (line 333). Popup windows are not preregistered, but the same registration-type information is provided to create a popup window (see Figure 3-2, page 42). This information is listed in the resource script file, PAYUP1.RC. The developer decides on the format of each dialog box, and either constructs the window using the AppStudio Dialog Editor (see Section 6), or enters educated guesses into a prototype dialog box listing in the PAYUP1.RC file to describe the window. (This type of dialog box "cloning" is more common when a series of dialog boxes must be prepared, and each one is approximately the same size. After the first dialog box is prepared, its template is copied below and modified to describe the next dialog box.) For now all dialog box templates will be provided to the developer; in Section 6 the developer will have the opportunity to create new dialog boxes.

For example, refer to lines 218 - 223: This is a popup dialog box template with the symbolic name CalcBox1. For manually created dialog boxes the symbolic name is used everywhere; the symbolic name is not defined in a "define" statement in PAYUP1.H. Not true for dialog boxes created in AppStudio Dialog Editor—see Section 6.

The word DIALOG identifies the box as a dialog box. This particular dialog box's top left corner is at these coordinates:

50 horizontal units to the right of the left edge of the screen,
0 vertical units down from the top edge of the screen.

The dialog box is 110 units wide and 55 units high. But what are the "units"? According to Rector 3.1, pp. 575-576, "A dialog statement primarily defines the position and size of the dialog box in dialog units. A dialog unit is 1/4 (horizontally) and 1/8 (vertically) of the system dialog base unit. A dialog base unit is derived from the size of a character in the system font. Windows uses dialog units, rather than pixels, to display a dialog box in the same relative size independent of the type of display used." See also Petzold 3.1, p. 413. The important point is that the dimensions placed in the dialog box template represent a fixed physical size *only* with respect to the font chosen for the dialog box. Each time the font changes (or font size), the dialog box physical size changes also.

Since the developer was requested to set the PC Windows display at "Standard VGA" before installing the Visual C++ Development System for Windows and this standard display is 640 pixels wide by 480 pixels high, some approximation of a "unit" can be made at this time, based on one particular font. Later, when PAYUP1 is executed, the first popup window that appears will be CalcBox1, and the window width will be approximately 58% of the total screen width. The window height will be approximately 27% of the total screen height. Since this popup window is 160 units wide by 60 units high, we conclude that the largest popup window that may be displayed is 275 units wide by 215 units high (even though there are 640 x 480 pixels on the screen). These numbers would change if the font used in the dialog box was changed from FONT 10 "Ms Sans Serif" (line 220). More of these approximation techniques will be shown in Section 6, the Dialog Editor.

The style of the dialog box is WS_DLGFRAME, which is a heavy-duty frame, but not as heavy-duty as the main window frame which uses WS_THICKFRAME. File WINDOWS.H, which is included at the top of every *.C file, also defines a thinner frame named WS_BORDER and an extended style frame named WS_EX_DLGMODALFRAME.

The dialog box has one line of text, "Popup #1," and one pushbutton. The word CTEXT means "center text." In later versions of PAYUP other keywords will be shown here, like LTEXT (left justified text), etc. The explanation of more of these terms will appear in the second windowed version of PAYUP.

97

To demonstrate the effect that the selected font has on dialog box size and placement, the developer should make the following source code changes after executing PAYUP1 a few times in its original form (Ref: Figure 5-3, file PAYUP1.RC):

- CalcBox2, line 226: Replace "Ms Sans Serif" with "MS Serif."
- CalcBox3, line 232: Replace "Ms Sans Serif" w "Times New Roman."
- CalcBox4, line 238: Replace "Ms Sans Serif" with "Courier."
- CalcBox5, line 244: Replace "Ms Sans Serif" with "System."

Recompile and rerun project PAYUP1 for each new case. Note the changes in dialog box size and placement caused by the change in font in each box. In each case the font size is "10." Try changing the font size to "12" or "8" in some of the dialog boxes, and even more changes in dialog box sizes will occur.

Message Boxes   The Message Box [Petzold 3.1, pp. 181-182, 443-445, Rector 3.1, pp. 583-585] is the simplest form of popup dialog box. It requires no registration, no template in a *.RC resource script file, and is included in a program with only one or two executable statements. It normally appears as the result of an "if" statement because the program is checking for an error in input or calculation. If the error occurs, the user is made aware of the problem through the message box. For example, project PAYUP2, Figure 5-4, page 119, lines 690-697:

```
690:     if(gMonPay <= gMinMonPay)
691:     {/* Pass through this window again */
692:     MessageBox(haDlg, "Monthly Payment too Low.  Try Again :,"
                 NULL, MB_OK | MB_ICONQUESTION);
693:     EndDialog(haDlg, TRUE);
694:     nCOUNTER = 4; /* Set up for Window #4 again */
695:     PostMessage(ghWnd, WM_COMMAND, IDM_CALC, OL);
696:     return TRUE;
697:     }
```

If the test in line 690 is TRUE, the message box statement displays the text "Monthly Payment Too Low. Try Again :" in a message box. For the message box, the font type, font size, box size, and box location on the screen are selected by the compiler. The argument "MB_OK | MB_ICONQUESTION" produces a pushbutton in the box and a large question mark. After the message box is displayed, the user must pick the OK pushbutton to continue the program. The PostMessage( ), line 695, sends the program back to an earlier dialog box (#4).

The message to be displayed in a message box need not be fixed text. By adding one more executable statement before the MessageBox( ) statement, active data can be entered into the message box. For example, to inform the user of the value of the integer LineLength, this form of message box is used:

```
sprintf(szTemp, "Line Length is %d bytes.," LineLength);
MessageBox(haDlg, szTemp, NULL, MB_OK);
```

where szTemp[ ] is declared as an ASCII string: char szTemp[xx].

The sprintf( ) statement is required because MessageBox( ) accepts only ASCII strings—no formatted text.

Do not write a great deal of information in the message box. If the ASCII string is too long the compiler places it in the box as two lines. Message boxes will appear throughout projects PAYUP2 and PAYUP3.

Naming the Owner of a Message Box   MessageBox( ) constructs may be used to perform either a single or a dual function:

- **Single (Passive) Function**   A message is only displayed to the user, with no "jump" in program execution. When the user picks the pushbutton, the developer expects program control to return to the next executable statement after the MessageBox( ) statement in the source code. Therefore the wParam value sent back to the owner of the message box is superfluous. In this case the named parent of the MessageBox( ) is usually the main window:

    MessageBox(ghWnd,"Ho Ho Ho",NULL,MB_OK);

    where "ghWnd" is the global handle name to the main window controlling procedure, WndProc( ). Recall that the MB_OK parameter dictates that an "IDOK" wParam value be sent to the message box owner with the message case WM_COMMAND. This scheme works so long as the developer does *not* place within the WM_COMMAND case in WndProc( ) a "wParam == IDOK" subcase. If, for some reason, the developer included the wParam == IDOK subcase in the WM_COMMAND case in WndProc( ), program control would jump there instead.

    If MB_OK may cause a problem in WndProc( ), use MB_CANCEL or MB_YES or MB_NO.

- **Dual (Active) Functions**   A message is displayed to the user, and program control is intentionally jumped to another source code area for further computation, etc. by the message box. In this case the handle name used as the first argument in MessageBox( ) is extremely important because it names the window controlling procedure to which program control will move to find a "WM_COMMAND message case" followed by a "wParam == XXX" subcase. The intent is to cause a "jump" in the program; the program does not return to the next executable statement after the MessageBox( ) construct.

PAYUP uses a compromise technique. The MessageBox( ) constructs are all single passive functions [program control always returns to the first executable statement after the MessageBox( )]. Then the jump to another area of the source code is commanded two lines later. The PAYUP series uses the passive message box technique because a logic variable named nCOUNTER must be set before any "jump" occurs.

Line-by-Line Description   The emphasis is placed on the sequencing of the six dialog boxes in PAYUP1. All the dialog boxes are empty. All references below refer to Figure 5-3, which began on page 87.

Assume that the main window in project PAYUP1 has been displayed and the main message loop (lines 337-340) is in operation. The "Begin" menu bar appears at the top left corner of the main window, below the "Payup Application" caption. The user picks **Begin|Start Payup Program....**

- Parameter wParam is set to IDM_CALC (PAYUP1.RC, line 207).
- A WM_COMMAND message is generated. WndProc( ) handles the message (line 405).
- The "else if" statement in WndProc( ), line 412, traps the message.
- Since nCOUNTER was set to 1 in line 334 in WinMain( ) during initialization, lines 414-418 in WndProc( ) are executed.
- Line 415 assigns a handle to procedure CalcProc( ).
- Line 416, DialogBox( ), calls CreateWindow( ) and creates dialog box CalcBox1, as formatted in file PAYUP1.RC, lines 218-223.
- DialogBox( ) issues a WM_INITDIALOG message which is trapped in procedure CalcProc( ), line 603.
- Since nCOUNTER = 1, line 606 is executed, which sets the user input focus to the pushbutton in the first popup dialog box (PAYUP1.RC, line 222).

TIP: The concept of visually "setting the focus" in a dialog box has no real significance until a dialog box is created with multiple controls that receive keyboard entry. In that case the program sets the focus to the editbox that requires the attention of the user first. The user may always choose to change the focus by picking another control with the mouse, however.

TIP: When WM_INITDIALOG returns TRUE it means that the windows system is expected to set the focus in the dialog box to the first active element encountered, or first element with the label WS_GROUP in the *.RC template. When WM_ INITDIALOG returns FALSE it means that the focus has already been set by a SetFocus( ) statement in the WM_INITDIALOG case, and windows need not set the focus.

- Popup dialog box #1 is displayed.

The user views Popup #1, which is empty except for an OK pushbutton. The user picks the pushbutton or depresses the Enter key (the IDCANCEL key), which issues a WM_COMMAND message to procedure CalcProc( ).

- The WM_COMMAND message is trapped at line 624.
- Line 627 in CalcProc( ) is satisfied, so line 628, EndDialog( ) executes, initiating closure of the dialog box.
- nCOUNTER is set to 2 in CalcProc( ) line 630. PostMessage( ), line 631, places a message in the main message queue, WinMain( ), lines 337-340. CalcProc( ) returns TRUE (line 632) to show successful completion of the procedure to DialogBox( ), line 416.
- Line 417, FreeProcInstance( ), frees CalcProc( ) procedure instance. WndProc( ) completes execution and returns control to the WinMain( ) main message loop.
- The message posted to the main message loop two steps earlier (by line 631) is now activated.
- The same execution sequence begins again, except that nCOUNTER = 2.

The user clicks through five empty windows (nCOUNTER = 1, 2, 3, 4, 5). Then on Popup #6 a choice is offered to the user:

Popup #6
Rerun Program ?

YES   NO

The focus has been set to the YES pushbutton because it is the first active element listed in the dialog box description (PAYUP1.RC, lines 248-255).

- nCOUNTER is reset to 1 just in case the user selects the YES pushbutton.
- If YES is selected, a new PostMessage( ), WM_COMMAND message is sent to the main message queue and the program begins all over again.
- If NO is selected, no PostMessage( ) is sent. Windows generates a WM_DESTROY message which is trapped in WndProc( ), line 449, and the program terminates.

The key statement in this series is the call to DialogBox( ) in procedure WndProc( ), which directs and sequences all of the lower-tier functions to display a dialog box in a format prescribed in the resource script file, PAYUP1.RC. As the developer will find in the second windowed version of PAYUP, the constructs under DialogBox( ), coupled with the format statements in the resource script file PAYUP.RC, allow the program to place data onto and remove data from the dialog box.

PAYUP2 SEQUENCE OF EVENTS

Load the PAYUP2 project into the VWB according to the New Project Loading Sequence found at the front of this book. Project PAYUP2 fills in the empty dialog boxes created in project PAYUP1. All references below refer to Figure 5-4, a listing of the *.DEF, *.H, *.RC, and *.C files in project PAYUP2, beginning at page 110.

In this second windowed version of PAYUP the emphasis is on:

- Writing data to and reading data from each dialog box
- Performing internal computation between window events
- Message box error messages

This version prints no hardcopy; that occurs in project PAYUP3. It is assumed that the developer has read and understands project PAYUP1, the initial windowed version of PAYUP. Table 5-1 on page 104 shows where code has been added to the initial version, PAYUP1, to produce the second version, PAYUP2.

The sequence of events does not change between the initial version and version two of PAYUP except that a seventh dialog box is added to allow recycling of the program. The user begins the process by picking **Begin|Start Payup Program...** at the main window.

Program control moves to WndProc( ), line 405, with wParam = IDM_CALC and nCOUNTER = 1.

Popup Dialog Box #1   This is the series of statements that creates, processes, and destroys dialog box #1.

- DialogBox( ) starts the creation process (line 416) by calling Create Window( ). The data in PAYUP2.RC, lines 218 - 226, the CalcBox1 template, is used to create the dialog box:

```
CalcBox1 DIALOG  50, 20, 160, 65
STYLE WS_DLGFRAME  |  WS_POPUP
FONT 10, "Ms Sans Serif"
{CTEXT "Program:  Payback Loan Monthly"      -1, 0,  5, 160, 8
 CTEXT "----------------------------------------"  -1, 0, 13,
                 160, 8
 CTEXT "This program computes the number of monthly" -1, 0, 25,
                 160, 8
 CTEXT   "payments required to pay off a loan." -1, 0, 35, 160, 8
 PUSHBUTTON "OK"                         IDOK, 64, 48, 32, 14
 }
```

- Four lines of centered text are prepared for entry into the dialog box.
- One OK pushbutton is set below the text.
- DialogBox( ) issues a WM_INITDIALOG message that is trapped at CalcProc( ), line 606 and 608. TRUE is returned in line 609 to show that the input focus should be set to the first active element—in this case the pushbutton.

Nothing happens until the user picks the pushbutton. This action issues a WM_COMMAND message to CalcProc( ) which is trapped at lines 642 and 644.

- EndDialog( ) is executed to begin closure of the dialog box and nCOUNTER is set to 2 (lines 646-647).
- A PostMessage( ) is sent to the main message queue (line 648) to be activated as soon as control is returned to WinMain( ), and TRUE is returned to show correct execution of proc CalcProc( ).
- WndProc( ) line 417 releases the handle to procedure CalcProc( ) and returns control to WinMain( ).

103

Table 5-1 (Changes to PAYUP1 to produce PAYUP2)

File and Section	Initial Version (PAYUP1) (Figure 5-3)	Second Version (PAYUP2) (Figure 5-4)
PAYUP.DEF	(No changes between versions)	(No changes between versions)
PAYUP.H	Lines 101-103	Lines 101-111 (define 8 additional symbolic names)
PAYUP.RC	Lines 201-255	Lines 201-282 (add 1 new dialog box, fill in existing boxes, and add an alternate format for Popup #4)
PAYUP.C		
1) Include statements	Lines 303-304	Lines 303-305 (include <std.lib> for computation and strings)
2) Declare global variables	Lines 308-310	Lines 309-314 (add global floats & strings to store calculations and displayed data)
3) WinMain( ) Initialize Computation	No change, line 334	No change, line 337
4) WndProc( )	Lines 412-446	Lines 412-451 (add a seventh dialog box)
5) AboutProc( )	(No changes between versions)	(No changes between versions)
6) CalcProc( ) Declarations, local variables	None	Lines 602-604 ("lhDummy" is a handle for the individual child window controls)
7) cases WM_INITDIALOG and WM_COMMAND	Lines 603-690	Lines 605-761 (changes too numerous to list—see text below)

Popup Dialog Box #2

- The PostMessage( ) in the main message queue is trapped in WndProc( ) line 419 and DialogBox( ) starts the creation process (line 421). The CalcBox2 template in PAYUP2.RC, lines 227-233, is used to create the dialog box:

```
CalcBox2 DIALOG 50, 26, 160, 65
STYLE WS_DLGFRAME  |  WS_POPUP
FONT 10, "Ms Sans Serif"
{CTEXT   "Enter Starting Loan Amount"         -1, 0,   5, 160, 8
EDITTEXT                       GETTEXT1, 60, 15, 34, 12,  SS_CENTER
PUSHBUTTON                         "OK"      IDOK, 64, 40, 32, 14
}
```

- One line of centered text is prepared for entry into the dialog box.
- One line of EDITTEXT is set below the static, centered text. This is a child window control, as is the pushbutton; it is a framed box into which the user types a reply.
- The last element is an OK pushbutton, set below the EDITTEXT box.
- DialogBox( ) issues a WM_INITDIALOG message that is trapped at CalcProc( ), line 610. To set the input focus to the EDITTEXT control, its handle is retrieved in line 612, the focus is set in line 613, and FALSE is returned to show that the focus is already set (default focus is not required).

TIP: The method for preloading data into any EDITTEXT control is demonstrated here. To preload this CalcBox2 EDITTEXT:

- Enable line 314B in Figure 5-4, which puts the amount 100000.00 (for example) into string DefaultText[ ].
- Enable line 610B, Set DlgItemText( ), which places the 100000.00 into GETTEXT1 before it is displayed in the CalcBox2 EDITTEXT control.

Note that the user need not use the preloaded data; it may be overtyped, then the OK pushbutton depressed. This same preload technique is shown in project SETUP1, Dialog Box #1, where the user chooses the name of the main directory to which the Book 1 source code is routed.

Nothing happens until the user enters the Loan Amount in the EDITTEXT box and picks the OK pushbutton. This action issues a WM_COMMAND message which is trapped at line 652.

- The "Loan Amount" entry is retrieved from the dialog box at line 654 and placed in ASCII buffer gLoanAmtBuf[ ]. In line 655 the ASCII answer is converted to a float, gLoanAmt.
- EndDialog( ) is executed to begin closure of the dialog box and nCOUNTER is set to 3. The next PostMessage( ) is placed in the main message queue. TRUE is returned.

QUESTION: Why were LoanAmtBuf[ ] (ASCII) and LoanAmt (FLOAT) declared as *global* variables?

ANSWER: If they were local variables they would lose their assigned values as soon as CalcProc( ) gave up program control. As soon as FreeProcInstance( ) is executed, all integer local variables in CalcProc( ) are set to zero. If a variable must "remember" its value from call to call, it must be a global variable or the values must be set into a "structure."

- WndProc( ) line 422 releases the handle to procedure CalcProc( ) and returns control to WinMain( ).

Popup Dialog Box #3

From this point on, the text will concentrate on the CalcProc( ) statements contained within the WM_INITDIALOG and WM_COMMAND cases. The dialog box #3 template is shown in PAYUP2.RC lines 234-241:

```
CalcBox3  DIALOG  50, 32, 160, 60
STYLE WS_DLGFRAME  |  WS_POPUP
FONT 10, "Ms Sans Serif"
  {CTEXT  "Enter Annual Interest Rate:"      -1, 0,   5, 160, 8
  CTEXT   "[ A number between 5.0 and 25.0 ] "  -1, 0, 15, 160, 8
  EDITTEXT                GETTEXT2, 60, 25, 40, 12,  ES_CENTER
  PUSHBUTTON                "OK"    IDOK, 64, 40, 32, 14
  }
```

- Two lines of centered text are prepared for entry into the dialog box, then one EDITTEXT is set below the text. The final element is an OK pushbutton.
- Control reverts to CalcProc( ) line 615. The focus is set to GETTEXT2 in line 617.

Nothing happens until the user enters the Interest Rate in the EDITTEXT box and picks the OK pushbutton. This action issues a WM_COMMAND message which is trapped at line 642.

- Control reverts to CalcProc( ) line 662.

- Line 664 places the user's answer in buffer gIntRateBuf[ ], and it is converted to float gIntRate in line 665.

- A test is made in line 667 to ensure that the interest rate is between 5.0 and 25.0 (not, for example, the number 0.07, which the user might enter to mean a 7 percent loan).

- If the interest rate is out of range, an error message is displayed on the screen to the user, "Interest Rate Out of Range. Try Again: ," lines 669. Then the program recycles to Popup #3 to receive new data as soon as the user clicks on the OK pushbutton in the message box.

- If the interest rate is within the 5.0 - 25.0 range, computation continues. A minimum monthly payment is computed (line 676), and converted to ASCII (line 678).

- The dialog process is complete so EndDialog( ) is executed and nCOUNTER is set to 4.

Popup Dialog Box #4

The dialog box #4 template is shown in PAYUP2.RC lines 242-250:

```
CalcBox4  DIALOG  50, 38, 160, 80
STYLE WS_DLGFRAME  |  WS_POPUP
FONT 10, "Ms Sans Serif"
  {CTEXT  "Minimum Monthly Payment Is:"      -1, 0,   5, 160, 8
  CTEXT  ""                      PUTTEXT1, 15,  40, 12,  SS_CENTER
  CTEXT  "Enter Monthly Payment:           -1, 0, 28, 160, 8
  EDITTEXT              GETTEXT3, 60, 40, 40, 12,  ES_CENTER
  PUSHBUTTON                "OK"   IDOK, 64, 60, 32, 14
  }
```

- Two lines of centered text are prepared for entry into the dialog box. The first line, "Minimum Monthly Payment Is:" is standard centered text, but the second line is new. The " " shows that no static text is to be placed here, but the ASCII data in PUTTEXT1 is to be printed instead. The PUTTEXT1 text will be assigned in the next WM_INITDIALOG statement.

- One line of centered text is prepared for entry into the dialog box, "Enter Monthly Payment:," then an OK pushbutton is placed below the text.

- Control reverts to CalcProc( ) line 620. The data in ASCII buffer gMinMonPayBuf[ ] is given an ID number PUTTEXT1 so it can be placed into the dialog box. Next, the focus is set to GETTEXT3.

Nothing happens until the user enters the Monthly Payment in the EDITTEXT box and picks the OK pushbutton.

- Control reverts to CalcProc( ) line 685.

- Line 687 places the user's answer in buffer gMonPayBuf[ ], and it is converted to float gMonPay in line 688.

- A test is made in line 690 to ensure that the monthly payment is greater than the minimum monthly payment.

- If monthly payment is too low, an error message is displayed on the screen to the user, "Monthly Payment Too Low. Try Again: ," line 692. Then the program recycles to Popup #4 to receive new data as soon as the user picks the OK pushbutton.

- If the monthly payment is high enough, computation continues in lines 699-709. The number of months required to pay off the loan is computed and the float answer (line 709) is converted to ASCII (line 711) for later display.

- The dialog process is complete so EndDialog( ) is executed and nCOUNTER is set to 5.

Popup Dialog Box #5

The dialog box #5 template is shown in PAYUP2.RC lines 251-266:

```
CalcBox5  DIALOG  50, 44, 160, 80
          STYLE WS_DLGFRAME  |  WS_POPUP
FONT 10, "Ms Sans Serif"
{CTEXT  "Entries:"                        -1, 0,   2, 160, 8
  CTEXT  "------------------------------------------------------"
         -1, 0, 10, 160, 8
  LTEXT  "Starting Loan Amount:            -1, 25, 15,  90,  8
  CTEXT  ""                        PUTTEXT2, 110, 15, 25,  8
  LTEXT  "Annual Interest Rate:"          -1, 25, 25,  90,  8
  CTEXT  ""                        PUTTEXT3, 110, 25, 25,  8
  LTEXT  "Monthly Payment:"              -1, 25, 35,  90,  8
  CTEXT  ""                        PUTTEXT4, 110, 35, 25,  8
  CTEXT  "All Entries Correct ? "         -1,  0, 48, 160,  8
  PUSHBUTTON                  "YES"    IDYES, 34, 60, 32, 14
  PUSHBUTTON                  "NO"     IDNO , 94, 60, 32, 14
  }
```

- Nine lines of text are prepared for entry into the dialog box. Six are static text and three are dynamic—PUTTEXT2, 3, and 4, which will be assigned in the next WM_INITDIALOG statement. Two pushbuttons are placed below the text.

- Control reverts to CalcProc( ) line 627. The data in ASCII buffer gLoanAmtBuf[ ] is given an ID number PUTTEXT2, buffer gIntRateBuf[ ] is assigned PUTTEXT3, and buffer gMonPayBuf[ ] is assigned PUTTEXT4 so they can be placed into the dialog box. Next, the focus is set to the first pushbutton encountered by returning TRUE.

Nothing happens until the user picks either the YES or NO pushbutton.

- Control reverts to CalcProc( ) line 718. If YES was selected the program prepares for case 6. If NO was selected the program recycles to case 2.

- The dialog process is complete so EndDialog( ) is executed and nCOUNTER is set to either 6 or 2.

Popup Dialog Box #6

The dialog box #6 template is shown in PAYUP2.RC lines 267-275:

```
CalcBox6  DIALOG  50, 50, 160, 60
STYLE WS_DLGFRAME  |  WS_POPUP
FONT 10, "Ms Sans Serif"
  {CTEXT  "Number of Months to Pay Off Loan Is:"-1, 0,  2, 160, 8
  CTEXT  ""                      PUTTEXT5, 60, 15, 40, 12, SS_CENTER
  CTEXT  "Rerun Program ? "                -1, 0, 27, 160, 8
  PUSHBUTTON                 "YES"    IDYES, 34, 40, 32, 14
  PUSHBUTTON                 "NO"     IDNO , 94, 40, 32, 14
  }
```

- Two lines of text are prepared for entry into the dialog box. Line 1 includes both a static text "Number of Months to Pay Off Loan Is: ," followed by the dynamic text in PUTTEXT5. Line 2 is all static text, "Rerun Program ? ." Two pushbuttons are placed below the text.

- Control reverts to CalcProc( ) line 633. The data in ASCII buffer ganswerBuf[ ] is given an ID number PUTTEXT5 so it can be placed into the dialog box. Next, the focus is set to the first pushbutton encountered by returning TRUE.

Nothing happens until the user picks either the YES or NO pushbutton.

- Control reverts to CalcProc( ) line 732. If YES was selected, the program prepares for case 7 and a complete recycle of the program. If NO was selected CalcProc( ) yields control and the program reestablishes the PAYUP main window.

Popup Dialog Box #7

The dialog box #7 template is shown in PAYUP2.RC lines 276-282:

```
CalcBox7 DIALOG 50, 56, 160, 60
STYLE WS_DLGFRAME | WS_POPUP
FONT 10, "Ms Sans Serif"
  {CTEXT "Use Same Loan Amount and Interest Rate ?"  -1, 0, 13,
            160, 8
  PUSHBUTTON                    "YES"    IDYES, 29, 30, 32, 14
  PUSHBUTTON                    "NO"     IDNO , 99, 30, 32, 14
  }
```

- One line of text is prepared for entry into the dialog box. Two pushbuttons are placed below the text (one YES, one NO).
- Control reverts to CalcProc( ) line 637. The focus is set to the first pushbutton encountered by returning TRUE.

Nothing happens until the user picks either the YES or NO pushbutton.

- Control reverts to CalcProc( ) line 746. If YES was selected the program prepares for case 4. If NO was selected the program prepares for case 2.

This completes the sequence of events for PAYUP2.

Book 1   Figure 5-4

```
Program PAYUP2 files:
  1. *.DEF, module-definition file
  2. *.H, header file
  3. *.RC, resource script file
  4. *.C,  WinMain( ), WndProc( ), AboutProc( ), CalcProc( aPROGRAM = )


/***************************************************************/

001: ; PAYUP2.DEF module-definition file -- used by LINK.EXE

002: ; ***************************************************
     ; *   This version of PAYUP uses:                  *
     ; *     1. Program entry via the main window MENU.  *
     ; *     2. Popup windows and message boxes.         *
     ; *     3. All logic except printing file at end.   *
     ; ***************************************************

003: NAME     Payup      ; Application's module name
004: DESCRIPTION  'Computes Number of Months to Pay Off a Loan'
005: EXETYPE WINDOWS   ;  Required for all Windows applications
006: STUB  'WINSTUB.EXE'; Generates error message if application
```

```
                         ;  is run without Windows
007: ;CODE can be moved in memory and discarded/reloaded
008: CODE   PRELOAD MOVEABLE DISCARDABLE
009: ;DATA must be MULTIPLE if program invoked more than once
010: DATA  PRELOAD MOVEABLE MULTIPLE
011: HEAPSIZE      1024


/*************************************************************/

101: /* PAYUP2.H (header file) */
102: #define IDM_ABOUT  10
103: #define IDM_CALC   15
104: #define GETTEXT1   51
105: #define GETTEXT2   52
106: #define PUTTEXT1   53
107: #define GETTEXT3   54
108: #define PUTTEXT2   55
109: #define PUTTEXT3   56
110: #define PUTTEXT4   57
111: #define PUTTEXT5   58


/*************************************************************/

201: /* PAYUP2.RC (resource script file) */
202: #include <windows.h>
203: #include "payup2.h"

204: PayupMenu MENU
205:   {POPUP        "&Begin"
206:     {MENUITEM "&About Payup...", IDM_ABOUT
207:     MENUITEM "&Start Payup Program...", IDM_CALC
208:     }
209:   }

210: AboutBox DIALOG 22, 17, 110, 55
211: STYLE DS_MODALFRAME | WS_CAPTION
212: CAPTION "About Payup"
213:   {CTEXT "Payup Application"            -1, 0,  5, 110,  8
214:   CTEXT "Microsoft Windows 3.1 and 4.0" -1, 0, 15, 110,  8
215:   CTEXT "Copyright \251 R. Braden, 1994" -1, 0, 25, 110,  8
216:   PUSHBUTTON "OK"                IDOK, 39, 36,  32, 14
217:   }

218: CalcBox1  DIALOG 50, 20, 160, 65
219: STYLE WS_DLGFRAME | WS_POPUP
220: FONT 10, "Ms Sans Serif"
221:   {CTEXT "Program: Payback Loan Monthly"           -1,0,
```

```
                 5, 160, 8
222:   CTEXT "----------------------------------------------"-1,0,
                13, 160, 8
223:   CTEXT "This Program Computes the Number of Monthly" -1,0,
                25, 160, 8
224:   CTEXT "Payments Required to Pay Off a Loan."        -1,0,
                35, 160, 8
225:   PUSHBUTTON "OK"                                     IDOK,64,
                48,  32, 14
226:   }


227: CalcBox2  DIALOG 50, 26, 160, 60
228: STYLE WS_DLGFRAME | WS_POPUP
229: FONT 10, "Ms Sans Serif"
230:   {CTEXT "Enter Starting Loan Amount:"  -1, 0, 5, 160, 8
231:   EDITTEXT  GETTEXT1, 60, 15, 40, 12,  ES_CENTER
232:   PUSHBUTTON "OK"    IDOK, 64, 40, 32, 14
233:   }


234: CalcBox3  DIALOG 50, 32, 160, 60
235: STYLE WS_DLGFRAME | WS_POPUP
236: FONT 10, "Ms Sans Serif"
237:   {CTEXT "Enter Annual Interest Rate:"      -1, 0, 5, 160, 8
238:   CTEXT "[ A number between 5.0 and 25.0 ]" -1, 0,15, 160, 8
239:   EDITTEXT GETTEXT2, 60, 25, 40, 12, ES_CENTER
240:   PUSHBUTTON "OK" IDOK, 64, 40, 32, 14
241:   }


242: CalcBox4  DIALOG 50, 38, 160, 80
243: STYLE WS_DLGFRAME | WS_POPUP
244: FONT 10, "Ms Sans Serif"
245:   {CTEXT "Minimum Monthly Payment Is:" -1,  0,  5, 160,  8
246:   CTEXT "" PUTTEXT1, 60, 15, 40, 12, SS_CENTER
247:   CTEXT "Enter Monthly Payment:"       -1,  0, 28, 160,  8
248:   EDITTEXT  GETTEXT3, 60, 40, 40, 12, ES_CENTER
249:   PUSHBUTTON "OK"               IDOK, 64, 60,  32, 14
250:   }


251: CalcBox5  DIALOG 50, 44, 160, 80
252: STYLE WS_DLGFRAME | WS_POPUP
253: FONT 10, "Ms Sans Serif"
254:   {CTEXT "Entries"             -1, 0,  2, 160, 8
255:   CTEXT "-----------------------------------------------"
256:        -1, 0, 10, 160, 8
257:   LTEXT "Starting Loan Amount:" -1, 25, 15,  90, 8
258:   CTEXT "" PUTTEXT2, 110, 15, 25, 8
259:   LTEXT "Annual Interest Rate:" -1, 25, 25,  90, 8
```

```
260:    CTEXT ""  PUTTEXT3, 110, 25, 25, 8
261:    LTEXT "Monthly Payment:"      -1, 25, 35,  90, 8
262:    CTEXT ""  PUTTEXT4, 110, 35, 25, 8
263:    CTEXT "All Entries Correct ?" -1,  0, 48, 160, 8
264:    PUSHBUTTON "YES"  IDYES, 34, 60, 32, 14
265:    PUSHBUTTON "NO"   IDNO , 94, 60, 32, 14
266:    }


267: CalcBox6  DIALOG 50, 50, 160, 60
268: STYLE WS_DLGFRAME | WS_POPUP
269: FONT 10, "Ms Sans Serif"
270:    {CTEXT "Number of Months to Pay Off Loan Is:" -1,0,5,160,8
271:    CTEXT "" PUTTEXT5, 60, 15, 40, 12, SS_CENTER
272:    CTEXT "Re-Run Program ?"                   -1, 0,27,160, 8
273:    PUSHBUTTON   "YES"                   IDYES,34,40, 32,14
274:    PUSHBUTTON   "NO"                    IDNO,94,40, 32,14
275:    }


276: CalcBox7  DIALOG 50, 56, 160, 60
277: STYLE WS_DLGFRAME | WS_POPUP
278: FONT 10, "Ms Sans Serif"
279:    {CTEXT "Use Same Loan Amount and Interest Rate ?" -1,0,13,
                 160, 8
280:    PUSHBUTTON   "YES" IDYES,  29, 30, 32, 14
281:    PUSHBUTTON   "NO"  IDNO,  99, 30, 32, 14
282:    }


/****************************************************************/

301: /* PAYUP2.C, R. Braden */
302: #define STRICT
303: #include <windows.h>
304: #include <stdlib.h>
305: #include "payup2.h"
306: long FAR PASCAL _export WndProc(HWND, UINT, WPARAM, LPARAM);
307: BOOL FAR PASCAL _export AboutProc(HWND, UINT,WPARAM,LPARAM);
308: BOOL FAR PASCAL _export CalcProc(HWND, UINT, WPARAM,LPARAM);
309: HANDLE  hInst;
310: HWND    ghWnd;
311: int  nCOUNTER;
312: /* Global variables to store floats/strings for "CalcProc"*/
313: double gLoanAmt, gIntRate, gMonPay, gMinMonPay, ganswer;
314: char gLoanAmtBuf[13], gIntRateBuf[13], gMonPayBuf[13],
        gMinMonPayBuf[13], ganswerBuf[13] ;

314A: /* Enable next line to preload data into Dialog Box #2 */
314B: /* char DefaultText[12] = "100000.00"; */
```

```
315:  int PASCAL
      WinMain(HINSTANCE hInstance,HINSTANCE hPrevInstance,
      LPSTR lpCmdLine, int nCmdShow)
316:  {MSG msg;
317:  WNDCLASS  wc;

318:  if(!hPrevInstance)
319:   {/* Main window */
320:   wc.style = NULL;
321:   wc.lpfnWndProc = WndProc;
322:   wc.cbClsExtra = 0;
323:   wc.cbWndExtra = 0;
324:   wc.hInstance = hInstance;
325:   wc.hIcon = LoadIcon(NULL, IDI_APPLICATION);
326:   wc.hCursor = LoadCursor(NULL, IDC_ARROW);
327:   wc.hbrBackground = GetStockObject(WHITE_BRUSH);
328:   wc.lpszMenuName =  "PayupMenu";
329:   wc.lpszClassName = "PayupWClass";
330:   RegisterClass(&wc);
331:   }

332:  hInst = hInstance;

333:  /* Create a main window for this application instance.  */
334:  ghWnd = CreateWindow("PayupWClass", "Payup Application",
       WS_OVERLAPPEDWINDOW, CW_USEDEFAULT, CW_USEDEFAULT,
       CW_USEDEFAULT, CW_USEDEFAULT, NULL,NULL,hInstance,NULL);

335:  ShowWindow(ghWnd, nCmdShow);
336:  UpdateWindow(ghWnd);

337:  nCOUNTER = 1; /* Start the program sequence */

337A:  /* Enabling the next statement causes the program to 'pick'
       the main  menu without  the user doing so.  Both menu list
       items are displayed when the main window becomes visible*/
       /* PostMessage(ghWnd, WM_SYSCHAR, 'B', 0x20000001); */

338:  while(GetMessage(&msg, NULL, NULL, NULL))
339:    {TranslateMessage(&msg);
340:    DispatchMessage(&msg);
341:    }
342:  return(msg.wParam); /* Returns value from PostQuitMsg */
343:  } /* End of WinMain( ) */

/***************************************************************/
```

```
401: long FAR PASCAL _export
     WndProc(HWND haWnd,UINT msg,WPARAM wParam,LPARAM lParam)
402:   {DLGPROC lpProcAbout;/* Pointer to "AboutProc" function */
403:    DLGPROC  lpProcCalc;/* Pointer to "CalcProc" function  */

404:   switch(msg)
405:     {case WM_COMMAND:
406:       if(wParam == IDM_ABOUT)
407:         {lpProcAbout=(DLGPROC)MakeProcInstance((FARPROC)
              AboutProc, hInst);
408:         DialogBox(hInst, "AboutBox", haWnd, lpProcAbout);
409:         FreeProcInstance((FARPROC)lpProcAbout);
410:         break;
411:         }
412:       else if(wParam == IDM_CALC)
413:         {switch(nCOUNTER)
414:           {case 1:
415:             lpProcCalc=(DLGPROC)MakeProcInstance((FARPROC)
                CalcProc, hInst);
416:            DialogBox(hInst, "CalcBox1", haWnd, lpProcCalc);
417:            FreeProcInstance((FARPROC)lpProcCalc);
418:            break;
419:           case 2:
420:             lpProcCalc=(DLGPROC)MakeProcInstance((FARPROC)
                CalcProc, hInst);
421:            DialogBox(hInst, "CalcBox2", haWnd, lpProcCalc);
422:            FreeProcInstance((FARPROC)lpProcCalc);
423:            break;
424:           case 3:
425:             lpProcCalc=(DLGPROC)MakeProcInstance((FARPROC)
                CalcProc, hInst);
426:            DialogBox(hInst, "CalcBox3", haWnd, lpProcCalc);
427:            FreeProcInstance((FARPROC)lpProcCalc);
428:            break;
429:           case 4:
430:             lpProcCalc=(DLGPROC)MakeProcInstance((FARPROC)
                CalcProc, hInst);
431:            DialogBox(hInst, "CalcBox4", haWnd, lpProcCalc);
432:            FreeProcInstance((FARPROC)lpProcCalc);
433:            break;
434:           case 5:
435:             lpProcCalc=(DLGPROC)MakeProcInstance((FARPROC)
                CalcProc, hInst);
436:            DialogBox(hInst, "CalcBox5", haWnd, lpProcCalc);
437:            FreeProcInstance((FARPROC)lpProcCalc);
438:            break;
```

```
439:        case 6:
440:          lpProcCalc=(DLGPROC)MakeProcInstance((FARPROC)
                CalcProc, hInst);
441:          DialogBox(hInst, "CalcBox6", haWnd, lpProcCalc);
442:          FreeProcInstance((FARPROC)lpProcCalc);
443:          break;
444:        case 7:
445:          lpProcCalc=(DLGPROC)MakeProcInstance((FARPROC)
                CalcProc, hInst);
446:          DialogBox(hInst, "CalcBox7", haWnd, lpProcCalc);
447:          FreeProcInstance((FARPROC)lpProcCalc);
448:          break;
449:          }
450:       break;
451:       }
452:     else
453:       return(DefWindowProc(haWnd, msg, wParam, lParam));

454:   case WM_DESTROY:
455:     PostQuitMessage(0);
456:     break;
457:   default:
458:     return(DefWindowProc(haWnd, msg, wParam, lParam));
459:     }
460:   return(NULL);
461:   } /* End of WndProc( ) */

/**************************************************************/

501: BOOL FAR PASCAL _export
     AboutProc(HWND haDlg, UINT msg, WPARAM wParam,LPARAM lParam)
502:   {switch(msg)
503:     {case WM_INITDIALOG:
504:       return TRUE;

505:     case WM_COMMAND:
506:       if(wParam == IDOK || wParam == IDCANCEL)
507:         {EndDialog(haDlg, TRUE);
508:         return TRUE;
509:         }
510:       break;
511:     }
512:     return FALSE;
513:   } /* End of AboutProc( ) */

/**************************************************************/
```

```
601: BOOL FAR PASCAL _export
     CalcProc(HWND haDlg, UINT msg, WPARAM wParam, LPARAM lParam)
602: {double AINT,AMT,PAYDOWN,fraction;
603: int KK;
604: HWND lhDummy;

605: switch(msg)
606:   {case WM_INITDIALOG:
607:     switch(nCOUNTER)
608:       {case 1:  /* This program calculates . . . */
609:         return TRUE; /* Set input focus to pushbutton */
610:       case 2:  /* Enter the loan amount . . . */
610A:        /* Enable next line to preload data into editbox*/
610B:        /* SetDlgItemText(haDlg,GETTEXT1,
                   (LPSTR)&DefaultText[0]); */
611:        /* Set input focus to keyboard entry GETTEXT1 */
612:        lhDummy = (HWND)GetDlgItem(haDlg, GETTEXT1);
613:        SetFocus(lhDummy);
614:        return FALSE;
615:      case 3:  /* Enter the interest rate . . . */
616:        /* Set input focus to keyboard entry GETTEXT2 */
617:        lhDummy = (HWND)GetDlgItem(haDlg, GETTEXT2);
618:        SetFocus(lhDummy);
619:        return FALSE;
620:      case 4:  /* Enter the monthly payment . . . */
621:        /* Post the calculated minimum monthly payment */
622:        SetDlgItemText(haDlg,PUTTEXT1,
                   (LPSTR)&gMinMonPayBuf[0]);
623:        /* Set input focus to keyboard entry GETTEXT3 */
624:        lhDummy = (HWND)GetDlgItem(haDlg, GETTEXT3);
625:        SetFocus(lhDummy);
626:        return FALSE;
627:      case 5:  /* Show entries . . . */
628:        /* Post the loan amt, interest, & payment */
629:        SetDlgItemText(haDlg,PUTTEXT2,
                   (LPSTR)&gLoanAmtBuf[0]);
630:        SetDlgItemText(haDlg,PUTTEXT3,
                   (LPSTR)&gIntRateBuf[0]);
631:        SetDlgItemText(haDlg,PUTTEXT4,
                   (LPSTR)&gMonPayBuf[0]);
632:        return TRUE;
633:      case 6: /* The number of months to pay loan is . .*/
634:        SetDlgItemText(haDlg, PUTTEXT5,
                   (LPSTR)&ganswerBuf[0]);
635:        /* Set input focus to first pushbtn in dlg box */
636:        return TRUE;
637:      case 7: /* Use same loan amount and interest rate */
```

```
638:            /* Set input focus to first pushbtn in dlg box */
639:            return TRUE;
640:          } /* End of switch (nCOUNTER) */
641:       break;

642:    case WM_COMMAND:
643:      switch(nCOUNTER)
644:        {case 1:  /* This program calculates . . . */
645:          if(wParam == IDOK || wParam == IDCANCEL)
646:            {EndDialog(haDlg, TRUE);
647:            nCOUNTER = 2; /* Set up the next popup window */
648:            PostMessage(ghWnd, WM_COMMAND, IDM_CALC, OL);
649:            return TRUE;
650:            }
651:          break;

652:        case 2:  /* Enter the loan amount . . . */
653:          if (wParam == IDOK || wParam == IDCANCEL)
654:            {GetDlgItemText(haDlg,GETTEXT1,
                   (LPSTR)&gLoanAmtBuf[0],12);
655:            gLoanAmt = atof(gLoanAmtBuf);
656:            EndDialog(haDlg, TRUE);
657:            nCOUNTER = 3; /* Set up the next popup window */
658:            PostMessage(ghWnd, WM_COMMAND, IDM_CALC, OL);
659:            return TRUE;
660:            }
661:          break;

662:        case 3: /* Enter annual interest rate . . . */
663:          if(wParam == IDOK || wParam == IDCANCEL)
664:            {GetDlgItemText(haDlg,GETTEXT2,
                   (LPSTR)&gIntRateBuf[0],12);
665:            gIntRate = atof(gIntRateBuf);

666:            /* Test that Interest Rate is between 5 & 25 */
667:            if((gIntRate < 5.0) || (gIntRate > 25.0))
668:              {/* Pass through this window again */
669:              MessageBox(haDlg,
                     "Interest Rate out of range.  Try Again :",
                     NULL, MB_OK | MB_ICONQUESTION);
670:              EndDialog(haDlg, TRUE);
671:              nCOUNTER = 3; /* Set up for Window #3 again */
672:              PostMessage(ghWnd,WM_COMMAND, IDM_CALC, OL);
673:              return TRUE;
674:              }

675:            /* Compute minimum monthly payment */
```

```
676:              gMinMonPay = gIntRate * gLoanAmt / 1200.;
677:              /* Put gMinMonPay into buffer gMinMonPayBuf */
678:              gcvt(gMinMonPay, 6, gMinMonPayBuf);
679:              EndDialog(haDlg, TRUE);
680:              nCOUNTER = 4; /* Set up the next popup window */
681:              PostMessage(ghWnd, WM_COMMAND, IDM_CALC, OL);
682:              return TRUE;
683:              }
684:         break;

685:         case 4: /* Enter the monthly payment . . . */
686:           if(wParam == IDOK || wParam == IDCANCEL)
687:              {GetDlgItemText(haDlg,GETTEXT3,
                     (LPSTR)&gMonPayBuf[0],12);
688:              gMonPay = atof(gMonPayBuf);
689:              /* Test that Monthly Payment > Minimum Payment*/
690:              if(gMonPay <= gMinMonPay)
691:                 {/* Pass through this window again */
692:                 MessageBox(haDlg,
                        "Monthly Payment too Low.  Try Again :",
                        NULL, MB_OK | MB_ICONQUESTION);
693:                 EndDialog(haDlg, TRUE);
694:                 nCOUNTER = 4; /* Set up for Window #4 again */
695:                 PostMessage(ghWnd,WM_COMMAND, IDM_CALC, OL);
696:                 return TRUE;
697:                 }
698:              /* Compute number of months to pay off loan */
699:              AMT = gLoanAmt;
700:              KK = 0;
701:              while(AMT >= 0.0)
702:                 {KK++;
703:                 AINT = AMT * gIntRate / 1200.;
704:                 PAYDOWN = gMonPay - AINT;
715:                 AMT = AMT - gMonPay + AINT;
706:                 }

707:              /* AMT is always a negative number */
708:              fraction = AMT / gMonPay;
709:              ganswer = KK + fraction;
710:              /* Convert "ganswer" to ascii */
711:              gcvt(ganswer, 5, ganswerBuf);
712:              EndDialog(haDlg, TRUE);
713:              nCOUNTER = 5; /* Set up the next popup window */
714:              PostMessage(ghWnd, WM_COMMAND, IDM_CALC, OL);
715:              return TRUE;
716:              }
717:         break;
```

```
718:        case 5: /* Show entries . . . */
719:          if(wParam == IDYES)
720:            {EndDialog(haDlg, TRUE);
721:             nCOUNTER = 6;
722:             PostMessage(ghWnd, WM_COMMAND, IDM_CALC, OL);
723:             return TRUE;
724:             }
725:          else if(wParam == IDNO || wParam == IDCANCEL)
726:            {EndDialog(haDlg, TRUE);
727:             nCOUNTER = 2;
728:             PostMessage(ghWnd, WM_COMMAND, IDM_CALC, OL);
729:             return TRUE;
730:             }
731:          break;

732:        case 6: /* Final answer has been displayed. */
733:          /* Rerun program ? */
734:          nCOUNTER = 7;/* Just in case a re-run requested */

735:          if(wParam == IDYES)
736:            {PostMessage(ghWnd, WM_COMMAND, IDM_CALC, OL);
737:             EndDialog(haDlg, TRUE);
738:             return TRUE;
739:             }
740:          else if(wParam == IDNO || wParam == IDCANCEL)
741:            {PostMessage(ghWnd, WM_DESTROY, O, OL);
742:             EndDialog(haDlg, TRUE);
743:             return TRUE;
744:             }
745:          break;

746:        case 7:/* Use same loan amount and interest rate ?*/
747:          if(wParam == IDYES)
748:            {EndDialog(haDlg, TRUE);
749:             nCOUNTER = 4; /* Set up next popup window */
750:             PostMessage(ghWnd, WM_COMMAND, IDM_CALC, OL);
751:             return TRUE;
752:             }
753:          else if(wParam == IDNO || wParam == IDCANCEL)
754:            {EndDialog(haDlg, TRUE);
755:             nCOUNTER = 2; /* Set up next popup window */
756:             PostMessage(ghWnd, WM_COMMAND, IDM_CALC, OL);
757:             return TRUE;
758:             }
759:          break;
760:        } /* End of switch(nCOUNTER) */
```

```
761:      break;
762:    } /* End of switch(msg) */
763:    return FALSE ;
764:  } /* End of CalcProc( ) */

/*************************************************************/
```

Figure 5-4   Project PAYUP

PAYUP3 SEQUENCE OF EVENTS

Load the PAYUP3 project into the VWB according to the New Project Loading Sequence found at the front of this book. All references below are to Figure 5-5, a listing of the *.DEF, *.H, *.RC, and *.C files in project PAYUP3. Figure 5-5 is shown at the end of this section, beginning at page 126. In this third windowed version of PAYUP the emphasis is on:

- Creating and writing to a file
- Reading from the file and printing its contents on a printer

Message boxes are used frequently in project PAYUP3 to warn the user of any errors that occur in file or printer procedures. A modeless dialog box is also used by the Print Abort system (recall that a modeless dialog box is one that, when created, need *not* be attended to by the user). Modeless dialog boxes are shown in greater detail in Book 2, *Child Windows*.

Windows programs work best using windows input/output functions (as opposed to the C 7.0 library non-window functions). As Petzold 3.1 states, pp. 750-751, "If you've ever written a simple formfeed program for MS-DOS, you know that ASCII number 12 activates a formfeed for most printers. Why not simply open the printer port using the C library function "open" and then output an ASCII number using "write"? Well, nothing prevents you from doing this. You first have to determine the parallel port or the serial port the printer is attached to—that's available from WIN.INI. You then have to determine if another program (the Print Manager, for instance) is currently using the printer. You don't want the formfeed to be output in the middle of a document, do you? Finally, you have to determine if ASCII number 12 is a formfeed character for the connected printer. It's not universal, you know. In fact, the formfeed command in PostScript isn't a 12; it's the word "showpage." In short, don't even think about getting around Windows; stick with the Windows functions for printing."

Mr. Petzold's advice should be heeded. But for this simple printing case the writer elected to demonstrate the exception to the rule: creating and printing a DOS file. Project PAYUP3 creates a DOS file, writes to the file, closes the file, then reopens the file and sends its contents to a printer. As the developer will soon discover, multiple conversions are required to switch between the DOS and Windows worlds, which makes the case for Mr. Petzold.

The reason for converting to DOS in this program is: The C library high-level stream input/output functions may be used to read to and write from the file rather than the lower-level Windows I/O functions. A later book in the Hands-On Windows Programming Series, Book 6, will deal with advanced printing techniques.

MS-DOS programs could write directly to the printer. Windows programs cannot. An intermediate file must be created, then its contents printed later.

There are additional reasons for including printing of a file in this book:

- Every developer should have a printing "package" that can be merged with new code to produce immediate printing capability, and this is one example (although it is old style and somewhat overdone).

- This book makes no statement about Microsoft Foundation Classes (MFC) techniques for prototyping and developing new software applications. But project PAYUP3 *does* make a statement, and the statement is: What a terrible way to include file printing capability into a simple program! Why not bundle-up all this additional code used solely for printing and call it into the project only at LINKing time to do its job? When the developer begins to ask these questions, she/he is starting to think in terms of the next generation of techniques: object-oriented code, foundation classes, unified input and output templates, etc.

File Procedures   The non-windows statement used to open a file, fopen( ), is replaced in windows programming with function OpenFile( ). OpenFile( ) is similar to fopen( ) except that it also maintains a structure of type LPOFSTRUCT (for example, Figure 5-5, line 769) to contain its CPU-to-disk operating system transport parameters. The developer makes no entries into this structure.

In project PAYUP3, the handle to the open file, hFile (Figure 5-5, line 769) is replaced immediately with a DOS file pointer pFile, using the conversion procedure fdopen( ), (line 777). This conversion enables the use of the high-level stream I/O procedures fread( ) and fwrite( ).

As the developer will recall, fprintf( ) places formatted text in a file while fwrite( ) places only ASCII strings in a file. Windows always requires two separate and distinct steps to write formatted text to any device:

- Convert formatted text to an ASCII string
- Write the ASCII string to the output device

Project PAYUP3 uses two statements to accomplish this task (for example, lines 791-792).

```
LineLength = sprintf(szTemp, "LOAN AMOUNT: %10.2f \x0D\x0A," AMT);
fwrite(szTemp, LineLength, 1, pFile);
```

The first statement puts the formatted text into an ASCII string "szTemp." The second statement writes the string to a DOS file whose file pointer is pFile. Note that if fdopen( ) is used in file opening, the C library function fclose( ) must be used to close the file.

If the "\x0D\x0A" symbols in line 791 appear strange, recall that this combination is represented in the C language as "\n," carriage return and line feed. There are no Tabs in the PAYUP3 text, "\t" —each Tab has been replaced with 8 blanks. Windows does not like "\n"s and "\t"s.

Windows writes to an output device one line at a time, and the windows program directs all line emplacement and line counting tasks—functions that DOS with PRINT.COM handled independently before.

In project PAYUP3 the "\x0D\x0A" are written to the DOS file to retain each end-of-record mark, just in case the user uses DOS to print the file later. If windows prints the file the "\x0D\x0A" confuse the text-transmitting process, and they are stripped off each record at print time.

Print Procedures Within Windows   Since Windows does not conceal its low-level printing attributes like DOS, most developers feel beholden to declare choices in these areas prior to printing:

- Font type and size
- Page size and orientation (portrait or landscape)
- Position of the text/graphics on the page

Fortunately Windows has defaults for two of the three above: The program will use an "MS Sans Serif," 12-point font on an 8.5 x 11 inch sheet of paper in the portrait orientation if no choices are made in the program. Windows will not automatically select the position of the text/graphics on the printed page, nor will it decide when it is time to skip to the next page (formfeed). These tasks are left to the developer.

Figure 5-5, the source listing for project PAYUP3, includes the four standard files: *.DEF, *.H, *.RC, and *.C, but it also contains three additional functions required to print or abort print, functions named GetPrinterDC( ), AbortProc( ), and AbortDlg( ), which were written by Microsoft for its demonstration program PRNTFILE. These three procedures appear at the end of the PAYUP3 source listing.

PAYUP3 Description   All line references below are to Figure 5-5. It is assumed that the developer has read and understands the contents of projects PAYUP1 and PAYUP2 where dialog and message boxes are used to control the flow of information to/from the user.

Within project PAYUP3, assume that the user has iterated on the program a sufficient number of times such that the final combination of inputs (amount of the loan, yearly interest rate, and proposed monthly payment) are correct at this time. At Popup dialog box #6 the answer has been displayed, "Number of Months Required to Pay Off Loan is: ____ ." In answer to the question, "Rerun Program ? ," the user has answered NO because all the answers are present. The program moves to Popup dialog box #8 and asks:

Print Amortization Table ?

The user picks the YES pushbutton. Control is transferred to line 765, case 8:

A file "PAYUP.NOW" is created in lines 768-782. The DOS file pointer is named "pFile," as declared in line 329.

- Nine lines of text are written to the file using the "sprintf/fwrite" combination in lines 784-804.
- A computational "while" loop is set up to compute the data, lines 805-812.
- To avoid "End of File" problems later, the characters "@@" are placed at the end of the DOS file, lines 813-815.
- The DOS file is closed, line 816.

File Printing in Windows

- The file to be printed is opened in lines 819-834.
- The "Printer Setup" dialog box, a common dialog box provided by Microsoft in library file COMMDLG.LIB is called in lines 835-840. The

developer has the option to "remark out" these lines and use the printer setup defaults.

- A handle to the "Device Context" is achieved in line 841, using the Microsoft function GetPrinterDC( ), lines A01-A31 at the end of Figure 5-5. The common dialog "print box" is presented to the user starting at line A10.

- Line 842 checks for receipt of a proper handle to the device context (the printer) by GetPrinterDC( ). If successful, the program continues. If not successful (!hPr) a message is sent to the screen to identify the problem, nCOUNTER is set to 1 for a restart, and the procedure is exited.

- Lines 848-853 and 919-924 have been "disabled" so the program uses a default 12 point Sans Serif font. The developer may choose other fonts by enabling these lines of code and entering a different font size and font name in lines 324 and 325.

If the developer changes the font or font size, it is best to monitor the result at lines 858-861, which are also disabled. These lines display the print parameters LineSpace, nPageSize, and LinePerPage. Using a 12 point MS Sans Serif font, the vertical line spacing is about 48 pixels (and most laser printers have 300 pixels/vertical inch). So 48 pixels produces about 6 lines of text/inch.

- Lines 854-857 determine nPage Size and LinesPerPage for the upcoming print.

- Lines 885-887 clear the printer for the upcoming print.

- Lines 888-895 read the first record from the file PAYUP.NOW and place it in ASCII buffer szTemp. Since the number of ASCII bytes in the text is unknown, the program reads one character at a time until the linefeed is encountered. ByteCounter counts the number of bytes in the ASCII string.

- LineLength = ByteCounter - 1 because the last byte read was the linefeed. What if the programmer neglected to put "\x0D\x0A" at the end of a record when the file was created? The file read command would fail!

- Lines 898-915 print the remainder of the file to the printer. The NEWFRAME command in function Escape( ) generates a formfeed.

- Lines 916-917 eject the last page from the printer and end the printing sequence (ENDDOC).

- Line 918 closes the file PAYUP.NOW.

- Lines 919-924 reset the printer defaults back to normal in Windows.

- Line 929 releases the Device Context. Printing is complete.

- Lines 930-933 display a "File 'PAYUP.NOW' Print Complete..." message and reset nCOUNTER to 1 for program recycling.

Print Abort in Windows   These are the necessary additions to provide a print abort capability in project PAYUP3. They include a modeless dialog box to allow the user to abort the print.

- An "abort print" dialog box has been added to file PAYUP3.RC, lines 289-297.
- The print abort functions are set up in lines 863-864.
- Line 866 activates the AbortProc( ) function.
- Lines 867-874 free the print abort functions if the print process fails to start.
- Lines 875-884 reset the print abort flag, then create and display the modeless print abort dialog box.
- Lines 925-928 free the print abort functions when the print process is complete.

This completes the description of PAYUP3.

PAYUP CLOSURE   If the developer understands the sequence of code necessary to proceed through the nine dialog boxes and three message boxes in the Payup project, then she/he is ready to take on this aspect of window programming. There are several voids that must be filled in the future, like how to deal with the larger class of logic elements such as the button classes, the listbox, the combo box, and scroll boxes. Printing from windows will continue to be a problem. Hopefully the next advance in programming, the use of "Foundation Classes" of code to implement specific software tasks, will take most of the drudgery out of printing, along with all other repetitive tasks that users perform within windows applications.

Book 1   Figure 5-5

```
Program PAYUP3 files:
1.  *.DEF, module-definition file
2.  *.H,   header file
3.  *.RC,  resource script file
4.  *.C,   WinMain( ),WndProc( ),AboutProc( ),CalcProc( ),
           GetPrinterDC( ),AbortProc( ),AbortDlg( ),

/*****************************************************************/
```

```
001: ; PAYUP3.DEF module-definition file -- used by LINK.EXE

002: ; ******************************************************
     ; *   This version of PAYUP uses:                     *
     ; *     1.  Program entry via the main window MENU.    *
     ; *     2.  Popup dialog box and message box windows.  *
     ; *     3.  Complete program, to include MS DOS file   *
     ; *             printing with print abort functions    *
     ; ******************************************************

003: NAME     Payup      ;  Application's module name
004: DESCRIPTION  'Computes Number of Months to Pay Off a Loan'
005: EXETYPE WINDOWS    ;  Required for all Windows applications
006: STUB  'WINSTUB.EXE';  Generates error message if application
                        ;  is run without Windows
007: ;CODE can be moved in memory and discarded/reloaded
008: CODE   PRELOAD MOVEABLE DISCARDABLE
009:;DATA must be MULTIPLE if program invoked more than once
010: DATA   PRELOAD MOVEABLE MULTIPLE
011: HEAPSIZE      1024


/***************************************************************/

101: /* PAYUP3.H (header file) */
102: #define IDM_ABOUT  10
103: #define IDM_CALC   15
104: #define GETTEXT1   51
105: #define GETTEXT2   52
106: #define PUTTEXT1   53
107: #define GETTEXT3   54
108: #define PUTTEXT2   55
109: #define PUTTEXT3   56
110: #define PUTTEXT4   57
111: #define PUTTEXT5   58

112: #define IDC_FILENAME  402

/***************************************************************/

201: /* PAYUP3.RC (resource script file) */
202: #include "windows.h"
203: #include "payup3.h"

204: PayupMenu MENU
205:   {POPUP        "&Begin"
206:     {MENUITEM "&About Payup...", IDM_ABOUT
```

```
207:    MENUITEM "&Start Payup Program...", IDM_CALC
208:       }
209:    }


210: AboutBox DIALOG 22, 17, 110, 55
211: STYLE DS_MODALFRAME | WS_CAPTION
212: CAPTION "About Payup"
213:   {CTEXT "Payup Application"              -1,  0,  5, 110,  8
214:    CTEXT "Microsoft Windows 3.1 and 4.0" -1,  0, 15, 110,  8
215:    CTEXT "Copyright \251 R. Braden, 1994" -1,  0, 25, 110,  8
216:    PUSHBUTTON "OK"                       IDOK, 39, 36, 32, 14
217:   }


218: CalcBox1  DIALOG 50, 20, 160, 65
219: STYLE WS_DLGFRAME | WS_POPUP
220: FONT 10, "Ms Sans Serif"
221:   {CTEXT "Program: Payback Loan Monthly"            -1,0,
              5, 160,  8
222:    CTEXT "----------------------------------------------"-1,0,
              13, 160,  8
223:    CTEXT "This Program Computes the Number of Monthly" -1,0,
              25, 160,  8
224:    CTEXT "Payments Required to Pay Off a Loan."        -1,0,
              35, 160,  8
225:    PUSHBUTTON "OK"                                    IDOK,64,
              48,  32, 14
226:   }


227: CalcBox2  DIALOG 50, 26, 160, 60
228: STYLE WS_DLGFRAME | WS_POPUP
229: FONT 10, "Ms Sans Serif"
230:   {CTEXT "Enter Starting Loan Amount:"  -1, 0, 5, 160, 8
231:    EDITTEXT  GETTEXT1, 60, 15, 40, 12,  ES_CENTER
232:    PUSHBUTTON "OK"    IDOK, 64, 40, 32, 14
233:   }


234: CalcBox3  DIALOG 50, 32, 160, 60
235: STYLE WS_DLGFRAME | WS_POPUP
236: FONT 10, "Ms Sans Serif"
237:   {CTEXT "Enter Annual Interest Rate:"     -1, 0, 5, 160, 8
238:    CTEXT "[ A Number Between 5.0 and 25.0 ]" -1, 0,15, 160, 8
239:    EDITTEXT GETTEXT2, 60, 25, 40, 12, ES_CENTER
240:    PUSHBUTTON "OK"  IDOK, 64, 40, 32, 14
241:   }


242: CalcBox4  DIALOG 50, 38, 160, 80
243: STYLE WS_DLGFRAME | WS_POPUP
```

```
244: FONT 10, "Ms Sans Serif"
245:   {CTEXT "Minimum Monthly Payment Is:" -1,  0,  5, 160,  8
246:    CTEXT "" PUTTEXT1, 60, 15, 40, 12, SS_CENTER
247:    CTEXT "Enter Monthly Payment:"      -1,  0, 28, 160,  8
248:    EDITTEXT  GETTEXT3, 60, 40, 40, 12, ES_CENTER
249:    PUSHBUTTON "OK"                IDOK, 64, 60,  32, 14
250:   }

251: CalcBox5  DIALOG 50, 44, 160, 80
252: STYLE WS_DLGFRAME | WS_POPUP
253: FONT 10, "Ms Sans Serif"
254:   {CTEXT "Entries"      -1, 0,   2, 160, 8
255:    CTEXT "-------------------------------------------------"
                 -1, 0, 10, 160, 8
256:    LTEXT "Starting Loan Amount:" -1, 25, 15,  90, 8
257:    CTEXT "" PUTTEXT2, 110, 15, 25, 8
258:    LTEXT "Annual Interest Rate:" -1, 25, 25,  90, 8
259:    CTEXT "" PUTTEXT3, 110, 25, 25, 8
260:    LTEXT "Monthly Payment:"  -1, 25, 35,  90, 8
261:    CTEXT "" PUTTEXT4, 110, 35, 25, 8
262:    CTEXT "All Entries Correct ?" -1,  0, 48, 160, 8
263:    PUSHBUTTON "YES"  IDYES, 34, 60, 32, 14
264:    PUSHBUTTON "NO"   IDNO , 94, 60, 32, 14
265:   }

266: CalcBox6  DIALOG 50, 50, 160, 60
267: STYLE WS_DLGFRAME | WS_POPUP
268: FONT 10, "Ms Sans Serif"
269:   {CTEXT "Number of Months to Pay Off Loan Is:" -1,0,5,160,8
270:    CTEXT "" PUTTEXT5, 60, 15, 40, 12, SS_CENTER
271:    CTEXT "Re-Run Program ?"             -1,0,27,160,8
272:    PUSHBUTTON   "YES"              IDYES,34,40,32,14
273:    PUSHBUTTON    "NO"              IDNO,94,40,32,14
274:   }

275: CalcBox7  DIALOG 50, 56, 160, 60
276: STYLE WS_DLGFRAME | WS_POPUP
277: FONT 10, "Ms Sans Serif"
278:   {CTEXT "Use Same Loan Amount and Interest Rate ?" -1,0,13,
               160, 8
279:    PUSHBUTTON    "YES" IDYES,  29, 30, 32, 14
280:    PUSHBUTTON     "NO"  IDNO,  99, 30, 32, 14
281:   }

282: CalcBox8  DIALOG 70, 62, 120, 40
283: STYLE WS_DLGFRAME | WS_POPUP
284: FONT 10, "Ms Sans Serif"
```

```
285:    {CTEXT "Print Amortization Table ?"            -1,0,6,120,8
286:    PUSHBUTTON    "YES"                    IDYES,14,20,32,14
287:    PUSHBUTTON    "NO"                     IDNO,74,20,32,14
288:    }

289: AbortDlg DIALOG 20,20,90, 64
290: STYLE DS_MODALFRAME | WS_CAPTION | WS_SYSMENU
291: CAPTION "PAYUP.NOW"
292: BEGIN
293:    DefPushButton "Cancel"       IDCANCEL,29,44,32,14,WS_GROUP
294:    Ctext    "Sending",           -1,        0,  8, 90,  8
295:    Ctext    "text",              IDC_FILENAME,0, 18, 90,  8
296:    Ctext    "to print spooler.", -1,        0, 28, 90,  8
297: END


/****************************************************************/


301: /*  PAYUP3, R. Braden */

302: /*  During the  LINKing  of this  program, an  additional */
     /*  library  file  "COMMDLG.LIB" is used.  It is  already */
     /*  included in the default linker. */

303: #define STRICT
304: #include "windows.h"
305: #include "print.h"
306: #include "commdlg.h"
307: #include "stdlib.h"
308: #include "io.h"
309: #include "stdio.h"
310: #include "string.h"
311: #include "payup3.h"

312: long FAR PASCAL _export WndProc(HWND, UINT, WPARAM, LPARAM);
313: BOOL FAR PASCAL _export AboutProc(HWND, UINT,WPARAM,LPARAM);
314: BOOL FAR PASCAL _export CalcProc(HWND, UINT, WPARAM,LPARAM);
315: HDC  FAR PASCAL _export GetPrinterDC(void);
316: int  FAR PASCAL _export AbortProc(HDC,int);
317: int  FAR PASCAL _export AbortDlg(HWND,unsigned,WORD,LONG);

318: HANDLE  hInst;
319: HWND    ghWnd; /* Global handle for main window */
320: int   nCOUNTER;

321: /* Font variables */
322: HFONT hFont, hFontOld;
323: int MapModePrevious;
```

```
324: int iPtSize = 12; /* Twelve point text */
325: PSTR pszFace = "MS Serif"; /* MS Serif font */

326: /* Print variables */
327: HDC hPr; /* Handle to printing device */
328: HFILE hFile; /* Windows file handle for "PAYUP.NOW" */
329: FILE *pFile; /* DOS file pointer for "PAYUP.NOW" */
330: int LineSpace,LinesPerPage,CurrentLine,LineLength,nPageSize;
331: char szTemp[81];
332: char szFileName[10] = "PAYUP.NOW";
333: OFSTRUCT OfStruct;
334: TEXTMETRIC TextMetric;

335: /* Variables from "common dialogs" */
336: OPENFILENAME ofn;
337: PRINTDLG pd;

338: /* Printer abort function variables  */
339: BOOL bAbort; /* FALSE if user cancels printing */
340: HWND hAbortDlgWnd;
341: DLGPROC lpAbortDlg, lpAbortProc;

342: /*Global variables to  store floats/strings for "CalcProc"*/
343: double gLoanAmt, gIntRate, gMonPay, gMinMonPay, ganswer;
344: char gLoanAmtBuf[13], gIntRateBuf[13], gMonPayBuf[13],
        gMinMonPayBuf[13], ganswerBuf[13] ;

345: int PASCAL
     WinMain(HINSTANCE hInstance,HINSTANCE hPrevInstance,
       LPSTR lpCmdLine, int nCmdShow)
346:   {MSG msg;
347:   WNDCLASS wc;

348:   if(!hPrevInstance)
349:     {/* Main window */
350:     wc.style = NULL;
351:     wc.lpfnWndProc = WndProc;
352:     wc.cbClsExtra = 0;
353:     wc.cbWndExtra = 0;
354:     wc.hInstance = hInstance;
355:     wc.hIcon = LoadIcon(NULL, IDI_APPLICATION);
356:     wc.hCursor = LoadCursor(NULL, IDC_ARROW);
357:     wc.hbrBackground = GetStockObject(WHITE_BRUSH);
358:     wc.lpszMenuName =  "PayupMenu";
359:     wc.lpszClassName = "PayupWClass";
360:     RegisterClass(&wc);
361:     }
```

```
362:    hInst = hInstance;

363:    /* Create a main window for this application instance. */
364:    ghWnd = CreateWindow("PayupWClass", "Payup Application",
            WS_OVERLAPPEDWINDOW, CW_USEDEFAULT, CW_USEDEFAULT,
            CW_USEDEFAULT, CW_USEDEFAULT, NULL,NULL,hInstance,NULL);

365:    ShowWindow(ghWnd, nCmdShow);
366:    UpdateWindow(ghWnd);

367:    /* Fill in non-variant fields of OPENFILENAME structure.*/
368:    ofn.lStructSize       = sizeof(OPENFILENAME);
369:    ofn.hwndOwner         = ghWnd;
370:    ofn.lpstrFilter       = NULL; /* szFilterSpec, not used */
371:    ofn.lpstrCustomFilter = NULL;
372:    ofn.nMaxCustFilter    = 0;
373:    ofn.nFilterIndex      = 1;
374:    ofn.lpstrFile         = szFileName;
375:    ofn.nMaxFile          = 20;
376:    ofn.lpstrInitialDir   = NULL;
377:    ofn.lpstrFileTitle    = NULL; /* szFileTitle;*/
378:    ofn.nMaxFileTitle     = 20;
379:    ofn.lpstrTitle        = NULL;
380:    ofn.lpstrDefExt       = "NOW"; /* Not used */
381:    ofn.Flags             = 0;

382:    /* Fill in non-variant fields of PRINTDLG structure. */
383:    pd.lStructSize = sizeof(PRINTDLG);
384:    pd.hwndOwner   = ghWnd;
385:    pd.hDevMode    = NULL;
386:    pd.hDevNames   = NULL;
387:    pd.Flags       = PD_RETURNDC|PD_NOSELECTION|PD_NOPAGENUMS;
388:    pd.nCopies     = 1;

389:    nCOUNTER = 1; /* Start the program sequence */

390:    while(GetMessage(&msg, NULL, NULL, NULL))
391:      {TranslateMessage(&msg);
392:      DispatchMessage(&msg);
393:      }
394:    return (msg.wParam); /* Returns value from PostQuitMsg */
395:    } /* End of WinMain( ) */

/****************************************************************/

401: long FAR PASCAL _export
```

```
       WndProc(HWND haWnd,UINT msg,WPARAM wParam,LPARAM lParam)
402:   {DLGPROC lpProcAbout;/* Pointer to "AboutProc" function */
403:   DLGPROC  lpProcCalc;/* Pointer to "CalcProc" function  */

404:   switch(msg)
405:     {case WM_COMMAND:
406:       if(wParam == IDM_ABOUT)
407:         {lpProcAbout=(DLGPROC)MakeProcInstance((FARPROC)
               AboutProc, hInst);
408:         DialogBox(hInst, "AboutBox", haWnd, lpProcAbout);
409:         FreeProcInstance((FARPROC)lpProcAbout);
410:         break;
411:         }

412:       else if(wParam == IDM_CALC)
413:         {switch(nCOUNTER)
414:           {case 1:
415:             lpProcCalc=(DLGPROC)MakeProcInstance((FARPROC)
                 CalcProc, hInst);
416:             DialogBox(hInst, "CalcBox1",haWnd, lpProcCalc);
417:             FreeProcInstance((FARPROC)lpProcCalc);
418:             break;
419:           case 2:
420:             lpProcCalc=(DLGPROC)MakeProcInstance((FARPROC)
                 CalcProc, hInst);
421:             DialogBox(hInst, "CalcBox2", haWnd, lpProcCalc);
422:             FreeProcInstance((FARPROC)lpProcCalc);
423:             break;
424:           case 3:
425:             lpProcCalc=(DLGPROC)MakeProcInstance((FARPROC)
                 CalcProc, hInst);
426:             DialogBox(hInst, "CalcBox3", haWnd, lpProcCalc);
427:             FreeProcInstance((FARPROC)lpProcCalc);
428:             break;
429:           case 4:
430:             lpProcCalc=(DLGPROC)MakeProcInstance((FARPROC)
                 CalcProc, hInst);
431:             DialogBox(hInst, "CalcBox4", haWnd, lpProcCalc);
432:             FreeProcInstance((FARPROC)lpProcCalc);
433:             break;
434:           case 5:
435:             lpProcCalc=(DLGPROC)MakeProcInstance((FARPROC)
                 CalcProc, hInst);
436:             DialogBox(hInst, "CalcBox5", haWnd, lpProcCalc);
437:             FreeProcInstance((FARPROC)lpProcCalc);
438:             break;
439:           case 6:
```

```
440:            lpProcCalc=(DLGPROC)MakeProcInstance((FARPROC)
                   CalcProc, hInst);
441:            DialogBox(hInst, "CalcBox6", haWnd, lpProcCalc);
442:            FreeProcInstance((FARPROC)lpProcCalc);
443:            break;
444:          case 7:
445:            lpProcCalc=(DLGPROC)MakeProcInstance((FARPROC)
                   CalcProc, hInst);
446:            DialogBox(hInst, "CalcBox7", haWnd, lpProcCalc);
447:            FreeProcInstance((FARPROC)lpProcCalc);
448:            break;
449:          case 8:
450:            lpProcCalc=(DLGPROC)MakeProcInstance((FARPROC)
                   CalcProc, hInst);
451:            DialogBox(hInst, "CalcBox8", haWnd, lpProcCalc);
452:            FreeProcInstance((FARPROC)lpProcCalc);
453:            break;
454:            }
455:          break;
456:          }
457:        else
458:          return(DefWindowProc(haWnd, msg, wParam, lParam));

459:      case WM_DESTROY:
460:        PostQuitMessage(0);
461:        break;
462:      default:
463:        return(DefWindowProc(haWnd, msg, wParam, lParam));
464:      }
465:    return(NULL);
466:    } /* End of WndProc( ) */

/****************************************************************/

501: BOOL FAR PASCAL _export
     AboutProc(HWND haDlg, UINT msg, WPARAM wParam,LPARAM lParam)
502:    {switch(msg)
503:      {case WM_INITDIALOG:
504:        return TRUE;

505:      case WM_COMMAND:
506:        if(wParam == IDOK || wParam == IDCANCEL)
507:          {EndDialog(haDlg, TRUE);
508:          return TRUE;
509:          }
510:        break;
511:      }
```

```
512:   return FALSE;
513:   } /* End of AboutProc( ) */


/*****************************************************************/

601: BOOL FAR PASCAL _export
     CalcProc(HWND haDlg, UINT msg, WPARAM wParam, LPARAM lParam)
602: {double AINT,AMT,PAYDOWN,fraction;
603: int KK , ByteCounter;
604: HWND lhDummy ; /* Handle to child window controls */
605: DWORD FlagSave; /* Printer setup variable */
606: char ch;

607: switch(msg)
608:   {case WM_INITDIALOG:
609:     switch(nCOUNTER)
610:       {case 1:  /* This program calculates . . . */
611:         return TRUE; /* Set input focus to pushbutton */
612:       case 2:  /* Enter the loan amount . . . */
613:         /* Set input focus to keyboard entry GETTEXT1 */
614:         lhDummy = (HWND)GetDlgItem(haDlg, GETTEXT1);
615:         SetFocus(lhDummy);
616:         return FALSE;
617:       case 3:  /* Enter the interest rate . . . */
618:         /* Set input focus to keyboard entry GETTEXT2 */
619:         lhDummy = (HWND)GetDlgItem(haDlg, GETTEXT2);
620:         SetFocus(lhDummy);
621:         return FALSE;
622:       case 4:  /* Enter the monthly payment . . . */
623:         /* Post the calculated minimum monthly payment */
624:         SetDlgItemText(haDlg,PUTTEXT1,
                 (LPSTR)&gMinMonPayBuf[0]);
625:         /* Set input focus to keyboard entry GETTEXT3 */
626:         lhDummy = (HWND)GetDlgItem(haDlg, GETTEXT3);
627:         SetFocus(lhDummy);
628:         return FALSE;
629:       case 5:  /* Show entries . . . */
630:         /* Post the loan amt, interest, & payment */
631:         SetDlgItemText(haDlg,PUTTEXT2,
                 (LPSTR)&gLoanAmtBuf[0]);
632:         SetDlgItemText(haDlg,PUTTEXT3,
                 (LPSTR)&gIntRateBuf[0]);
633:         SetDlgItemText(haDlg,PUTTEXT4,
                 (LPSTR)&gMonPayBuf[0]);
634:         return TRUE;
635:       case 6: /* The number of months to pay loan is . .*/
636:         SetDlgItemText(haDlg, PUTTEXT5,
```

```
                   (LPSTR)&ganswerBuf[0]);
637:          /* Set input focus to first pushbtn in dlg box */
638:          return TRUE;
639:        case 7: /* Use same loan amount and interest rate */
640:          /* Set input focus to first pushbtn in dlg box */
641:          return TRUE;
642:        case 8:  /* Print amortization list ? */
643:          return TRUE;
644:        } /* End of switch(nCOUNTER) */
645:      break;

646:    case WM_COMMAND:
647:      switch(nCOUNTER)
648:        {case 1:  /* This program calculates . . . */
649:          if(wParam == IDOK || wParam == IDCANCEL)
650:            {EndDialog(haDlg, TRUE);
651:            nCOUNTER = 2; /* Set up the next popup window */
652:            PostMessage(ghWnd, WM_COMMAND, IDM_CALC, OL);
653:            return TRUE;
654:            }
655:          break;

656:        case 2:  /* Enter the loan amount . . . */
657:          if(wParam == IDOK || wParam == IDCANCEL)
658:            {GetDlgItemText(haDlg, GETTEXT1,
                   (LPSTR)&gLoanAmtBuf[0],12);
659:            gLoanAmt = atof(gLoanAmtBuf);
660:            EndDialog(haDlg, TRUE);
661:            nCOUNTER = 3;
662:            PostMessage(ghWnd, WM_COMMAND, IDM_CALC, OL);
663:            return TRUE;
664:            }
665:          break;

666:        case 3: /* Enter annual interest rate . . . */
667:          if(wParam == IDOK || wParam == IDCANCEL)
668:            {GetDlgItemText(haDlg, GETTEXT2,
                   (LPSTR)&gIntRateBuf[0],12);
669:            gIntRate = atof(gIntRateBuf);

670:            /* Test that Interest Rate is between 5 & 25 */
671:            if((gIntRate < 5.0) || (gIntRate > 25.0))
672:              {/* Pass through this window again */
673:              MessageBox(haDlg,
                   "Interest Rate out of range.  Try Again :",
                   NULL, MB_OK | MB_ICONQUESTION);
674:              EndDialog(haDlg, TRUE);
```

```
675:                    nCOUNTER = 3; /* Set up for Window #3 again */
676:                    PostMessage(ghWnd,WM_COMMAND, IDM_CALC, OL);
677:                    return TRUE;
678:                    }

679:                /* Compute minimum monthly payment */
680:                gMinMonPay = gIntRate * gLoanAmt / 1200.;
681:                /* Put gMinMonPay into buffer gMinMonPayBuf */
682:                gcvt(gMinMonPay, 6, gMinMonPayBuf);
683:                EndDialog(haDlg, TRUE);
684:                nCOUNTER = 4;
685:                PostMessage(ghWnd, WM_COMMAND, IDM_CALC, OL);
686:                return TRUE;
687:                }
688:           break;

689:       case 4: /* Enter the monthly payment . . . */
690:           if(wParam == IDOK || wParam == IDCANCEL)
691:               {GetDlgItemText(haDlg, GETTEXT3,
                      (LPSTR)&gMonPayBuf[0],12);
692:                gMonPay = atof(gMonPayBuf);

693:                /* Test that Monthly Payment > Minimum Payment*/
694:                if(gMonPay <= gMinMonPay)
695:                   {/* Pass through this window again */
696:                    MessageBox(haDlg,
                          "Monthly Payment too Low.  Try Again :",
                          NULL, MB_OK | MB_ICONQUESTION);
697:                    EndDialog(haDlg, TRUE);
698:                    nCOUNTER = 4; /* Set up for Window #4 again */
699:                    PostMessage(ghWnd,WM_COMMAND, IDM_CALC, OL);
700:                    return TRUE;
701:                    }

702:                /* Compute number of months to pay off loan */
703:                AMT = gLoanAmt;
704:                KK = 0;
705:                while(AMT >= 0.0)
706:                   {KK++;
707:                    AINT = AMT * gIntRate / 1200.;
708:                    PAYDOWN = gMonPay - AINT;
709:                    AMT = AMT - gMonPay + AINT;
710:                    }

711:                /* AMT is always a negative number */
712:                fraction = AMT / gMonPay;
713:                ganswer = KK + fraction;
```

137

```
714:                /* Convert "ganswer" to ascii */
715:                gcvt(ganswer, 5, ganswerBuf);
716:                EndDialog(haDlg, TRUE);
717:                nCOUNTER = 5;
718:                PostMessage(ghWnd, WM_COMMAND, IDM_CALC, OL);
719:                return TRUE;
720:                }
721:            break;

722:         case 5: /* Show entries . . . */
723:            if(wParam == IDYES)
724:              {EndDialog(haDlg, TRUE);
725:               nCOUNTER = 6;
726:               PostMessage(ghWnd, WM_COMMAND, IDM_CALC, OL);
727:               return TRUE;
728:               }
729:            else if(wParam == IDNO || wParam == IDCANCEL)
730:              {EndDialog(haDlg, TRUE);
731:               nCOUNTER = 2;
732:               PostMessage(ghWnd, WM_COMMAND, IDM_CALC, OL);
733:               return TRUE;
734:               }
735:            break;

736:         case 6: /* Final answer has been displayed. */
737:            /* Rerun program ? */
738:            if(wParam == IDYES)
739:              {nCOUNTER = 7; /* Set up next popup window */
740:               PostMessage(ghWnd, WM_COMMAND, IDM_CALC, OL);
741:               EndDialog(haDlg, TRUE);
742:               return TRUE;
743:               }
744:            else if(wParam == IDNO || wParam == IDCANCEL)
745:              {nCOUNTER = 8;
746:               PostMessage(ghWnd, WM_COMMAND, IDM_CALC, OL);
747:               EndDialog(haDlg, TRUE);
748:               return TRUE;
749:               }
750:            break;

751:         case 7: /* Use same loan amount and interest rate ?*/
752:            if(wParam == IDYES)
753:              {EndDialog(haDlg, TRUE);
754:               nCOUNTER = 4; /* Return to popup window #4 */
755:               PostMessage(ghWnd, WM_COMMAND, IDM_CALC, OL);
756:               return TRUE;
757:               }
```

```
758:            else if(wParam == IDNO || wParam == IDCANCEL)
759:              {EndDialog(haDlg, TRUE);
760:              nCOUNTER = 2; /* Return to popup window #2 */
761:              PostMessage(ghWnd, WM_COMMAND, IDM_CALC, OL);
762:              return TRUE;
763:              }
764:            break;

765:          case 8: /* Print hardcopy ? */
766:            if(wParam == IDYES)
767:              {EndDialog(haDlg, TRUE);
768:              /* Open a temporary file, "PAYUP.NOW" */
769:              if((hFile = OpenFile((LPSTR)szFileName,
                      (LPOFSTRUCT)&OfStruct, OF_CREATE)) == NULL)
770:                {sprintf(szTemp,
                  "Can't open file 'PAYUP.NOW' to record output.");
771:              MessageBox(ghWnd, szTemp, NULL,MB_OK | MB_ICONHAND);
772:                nCOUNTER = 1; /* Start all over again */
773:                return TRUE;
774:                }
775:              else
776:                {/* Convert window file hndl to DOS file ptr*/
777:                if((pFile = fdopen(hFile,"w+")) == NULL)
778:                  {sprintf(szTemp,
                    "Can't open file 'PAYUP.NOW' for DOS format.");
779:              MessageBox(ghWnd,szTemp,NULL,MB_OK | MB_ICONHAND);
780:                  nCOUNTER = 1; /* Start all over again */
781:                  return TRUE;
782:                  }
783:                }

784:      /* File "PAYUP.NOW" is open, ready to receive data */
785:      KK = 0; AINT = 0.0; PAYDOWN = 0.0; AMT = gLoanAmt;
786:      /* Replace all "\n" with "\x0D\x0A" for DOS file prtg
            Windows doesn't like TABs either; use 8 blanks */
787:      LineLength = sprintf(szTemp, "PAYUP PROGRAM: \x0D\x0A");
788:      fwrite(szTemp, LineLength, 1, pFile);
789:      LineLength = sprintf(szTemp, "-------------\x0D\x0A");
790:      fwrite(szTemp, LineLength, 1, pFile);
791:      LineLength = sprintf(szTemp,
    "                    LOAN AMOUNT:   %10.2f\x0D\x0A",AMT);
792:      fwrite(szTemp, LineLength, 1, pFile);
793:      LineLength = sprintf(szTemp,
    "                       INTEREST RATE:   %7.3f\x0D\x0A",
            gIntRate);
794:      fwrite(szTemp, LineLength, 1, pFile);
795:      LineLength = sprintf(szTemp,
```

```
     "                                   MONTHLY PAYMENT:  %7.2f\x0D\x0A",
            gMonPay);
796:    fwrite(szTemp, LineLength, 1, pFile);
797:    LineLength = sprintf(szTemp," \x0D\x0A");
798:    fwrite(szTemp, LineLength, 1, pFile);
799:    LineLength = sprintf(szTemp,
     "          NUM.   PAYMENT   INTEREST   PAYDOWN   NEW PRINCI
            PLE\x0D\x0A");
800:    fwrite(szTemp, LineLength, 1, pFile);
801:    LineLength = sprintf(szTemp,
     "          ----  ---------  --------  ---------  ----------
            ---\x0D\x0A");
802:    fwrite(szTemp, LineLength, 1, pFile);
803:    LineLength = sprintf(szTemp,
     "              %3d                                    %9.2f\x0
            D\x0A",
              KK,AMT);
804:    fwrite(szTemp, LineLength, 1, pFile);

805:    while(AMT >= 0.0)
806:      {KK++;
807:      AINT = AMT * gIntRate / 1200.;
808:      PAYDOWN = gMonPay - AINT;
809:      AMT = AMT - gMonPay + AINT;
810:      LineLength = sprintf(szTemp,
     "              %3d  %9.2f  %9.2f  %9.2f    %9.2f\x0D\x0A",
              KK, gMonPay, AINT, PAYDOWN, AMT);
811:      fwrite(szTemp, LineLength, 1, pFile);
812:      }

813:             /*"End of File" troubles.Use "aa" to show EOF.*/
814:             LineLength = sprintf(szTemp,"aa\x0D\x0A");
815:             fwrite(szTemp, LineLength, 1, pFile);
816:             fclose(pFile);
817:             /* All data is in file "PAYUP.NOW" */
818:             /* Print a DOS file, via windows */

819:             /* Open DOS file, "PAYUP.NOW" */
820:             if((hFile = OpenFile((LPSTR)szFileName,
                 (LPOFSTRUCT)&OfStruct, OF_READ)) == NULL)
821:                {sprintf(szTemp,
                 "Can't re-open file 'PAYUP.NOW' for printing.");
822:             MessageBox(ghWnd,szTemp,NULL,MB_OK | MB_ICONHAND);
823:                nCOUNTER = 1; /* Start all over again */
824:                return TRUE;
825:                }
826:             else
```

```
827:              {/* Convert window file hndl to DOS file ptr*/
828:              if((pFile = fdopen(hFile, "r")) == NULL)
829:                {sprintf(szTemp,
              "Can't re-open file 'PAYUP.NOW' to DOS format.");
830:         MessageBox(ghWnd,szTemp,NULL,MB_OK | MB_ICONHAND);
831:              nCOUNTER = 1; /* Start all over again */
832:              return TRUE;
833:                }
834:              }

835:          /* Printer Setup, OPTION #1 */
836:          FlagSave = pd.Flags;
837:          pd.Flags |= PD_PRINTSETUP;
838:          PrintDlg((LPPRINTDLG)&pd);
839:          pd.Flags = FlagSave;
840:          /* End of printer setup option */

841:          hPr = GetPrinterDC( );   /* Local function */
842:          if(!hPr)
843:            {sprintf(szTemp, "Cannot get Device Context.",
                  NULL, MB_OK);
844:         MessageBox(ghWnd,szTemp,NULL,MB_OK | MB_ICONHAND);
845:              nCOUNTER = 1; /* Start all over again */
846:              return TRUE;
847:              }

848:          /* Set font, OPTION #2, PART ONE
849:          MapModePrevious = SetMapMode(hPr, MM_TWIPS);
850:          hFont = CreateFont(-iPtSize * 3,0,0,0,0,0,0,0,0,
851:              0,0,0,0, pszFace);
852:          hFontOld = SelectObject(hPr, hFont);
853:              End of set font option, PART ONE */

854:          GetTextMetrics(hPr, &TextMetric);
855:          LineSpace = TextMetric.tmHeight +
                  TextMetric.tmExternalLeading;
856:          nPageSize = GetDeviceCaps(hPr, VERTRES);
857:          LinesPerPage = nPageSize / LineSpace - 1;

858:          /* TextMetrics check, Option #3
859:          sprintf(szTemp,
                  "LSpace, nPageS, LinesPP = %d, %d, %d.",
                  LineSpace, nPageSize, LinesPerPage);
860:          MessageBox(ghWnd, szTemp, NULL, MB_OK);
861:              End of TextMetrics check, Option #3 */

862:          /* Set up print abort functions */
```

```
863:              lpAbortDlg=(DLGPROC)MakeProcInstance((FARPROC)
                   AbortDlg, hInst);
864:              lpAbortProc=(DLGPROC)MakeProcInstance((FARPROC)
                   AbortProc, hInst);

865:              /* Define the abort function */
866:              Escape(hPr, SETABORTPROC, NULL,(LPSTR)
                   lpAbortProc, (LPSTR) NULL);

867:              if(Escape(hPr, STARTDOC, 0, 0L,(LPSTR)NULL) < 0)
868:                {MessageBox(ghWnd,"Unable to Start Print Job.",
                     NULL, MB_OK | MB_ICONHAND);
869:                 FreeProcInstance((FARPROC)lpAbortDlg);
870:                 FreeProcInstance((FARPROC)lpAbortProc);
871:                 DeleteDC(hPr);
872:                 nCOUNTER = 1; /* Start all over again */
873:                 return TRUE;
874:                }

875:              bAbort = FALSE; /* Clear the abort flag */

876:              /* Create the Abort dialog box (modeless) */
877:              hAbortDlgWnd = CreateDialog(hInst, "AbortDlg",
878:                ghWnd, lpAbortDlg);

879:              if(!hAbortDlgWnd)
880:                {MessageBox(ghWnd, "NULL Abort window handle",
                     NULL, MB_OK | MB_ICONHAND);
881:                 return (FALSE);
882:                }

883:              /* Now show Abort dialog */
884:              ShowWindow(hAbortDlgWnd, SW_NORMAL);

885:              /* Print empty page 1; else print doesn't work*/
886:              Escape(hPr, NEWFRAME, 0, 0L, 0L);
887:              CurrentLine = 1;

888:              /*Read 1 char at a time; string length unknown*/
889:              ByteCounter = 0;
890:              ch = fgetc(pFile);
891:              while(ch != '\x0A') /* Linefeed */
892:                {szTemp[ByteCounter] = ch;
893:                 ByteCounter++;
894:                 ch = fgetc(pFile);
895:                }
896:              /* First line  is now  in string  "szTemp", less
```

carriage controls. Send TextOut( ) pure text
since printing occurs one line at a time in windows. Exclude "\xOD\xOA" by setting LineLength
at ByteCounter -1. */

```
897:        LineLength = ByteCounter - 1;

898:        /* Main printing loop;uses pseudo EOF to quit */
899:        while((szTemp[0] != 'a') && (szTemp[1] != 'a'))
900:           {TextOut(hPr,0,CurrentLine * LineSpace,
                  (LPSTR)szTemp, LineLength);

901:           if(CurrentLine >= LinesPerPage)
902:             {Escape(hPr, NEWFRAME, 0, OL, OL);
903:             CurrentLine = 1;
904:             }
905:           else CurrentLine++;

906:           /* Read next line from file */
907:           ByteCounter = 0;
908:           ch = fgetc(pFile);
909:           while(ch != '\xOA') /* Linefeed */
910:             {szTemp[ByteCounter] = ch;
911:             ByteCounter++;
912:             ch = fgetc(pFile);
913:             }
914:           LineLength = ByteCounter - 1;
915:           } /* End of main printing loop */

916:        Escape(hPr, NEWFRAME, 0, OL, OL);
917:        Escape(hPr, ENDDOC, 0, OL, OL);

918:        fclose(pFile); /* Close DOS file "PAYUP.NOW" */

919:        /* Set font, Option #2, PART TWO */
920:        /* Reset printer front to old default
921:        SetMapMode(hPr, MapModePrevious);
922:        SelectObject(hPr, hFontOld);
923:        DeleteObject(hFont);
924:        End of set font option, PART TWO */

925:        /* Destroy the Abort Dialog Box */
926:        DestroyWindow(hAbortDlgWnd);
927:        FreeProcInstance((FARPROC)lpAbortDlg);
928:        FreeProcInstance((FARPROC)lpAbortProc);

929:        DeleteDC(hPr); /* Release Printer */
```

```
930:            sprintf(szTemp,
                "File 'PAYUP.NOW' Print Complete . .");
931:            MessageBox(ghWnd,szTemp,"PAYUP PROGRAM",
                MB_OK | MB_ICONINFORMATION);
932:            nCOUNTER = 1; /* Recycle to start */
933:            return TRUE;
934:            }
935:          else if(wParam == IDNO || wParam == IDCANCEL)
936:            {EndDialog(haDlg, TRUE);
937:            nCOUNTER = 1; /* Recycle to start */
938:            return TRUE;
939:            }
940:          break;
941:        } /* End of switch(nCOUNTER) */
942:      break;
943:    } /* End of switch(msg) */
944:  return FALSE ;
945:  } /* End of CalcProc( ) */


/****************************************************************

A01:  FUNCTION: GetPrinterDC( ) [MS function from "Prntfile"]

      PURPOSE: Get hDC for current device on current output port
               according to info in WIN.INI.
      COMMENTS:
          Searches WIN.INI for information about what printer is
          connected, and if found, creates a DC for the printer.
            returns
              hDC > 0 if success
              hDC = 0 if failure
****************************************************************/

A02: HDC FAR PASCAL _export
     GetPrinterDC(void)
A03:   {HDC          hDC;
A04:   LPDEVMODE    lpDevMode = NULL;
A05:   LPDEVNAMES   lpDevNames;
A06:   LPSTR        lpszDriverName;
A07:   LPSTR        lpszDeviceName;
A08:   LPSTR        lpszPortName;

A09:   if(!PrintDlg((LPPRINTDLG)&pd)) return(NULL);

A10:   if(pd.hDC) hDC = pd.hDC;
A11:   else
A12:     {if(!pd.hDevNames) return(NULL);
```

```
A13:    lpDevNames = (LPDEVNAMES)GlobalLock(pd.hDevNames);
A14:    lpszDriverName =
            (LPSTR)lpDevNames + lpDevNames->wDriverOffset;
A15:    lpszDeviceName =
            (LPSTR)lpDevNames + lpDevNames->wDeviceOffset;
A16:    lpszPortName   =
            (LPSTR)lpDevNames + lpDevNames->wOutputOffset;
A17:    GlobalUnlock(pd.hDevNames);

A18:    if(pd.hDevMode) lpDevMode =
            (LPDEVMODE)GlobalLock(pd.hDevMode);

A19:    hDC=CreateDC(lpszDriverName,lpszDeviceName,lpszPortName,
            (LPSTR)lpDevMode);

A20:    if(pd.hDevMode && lpDevMode) GlobalUnlock(pd.hDevMode);
A21:    }

A22:   if(pd.hDevNames)
A23:    {GlobalFree(pd.hDevNames);
A24:    pd.hDevNames = NULL;
A25:    }
A26:   if(pd.hDevMode)
A27:    {GlobalFree(pd.hDevMode);
A28:    pd.hDevMode = NULL;
A29:    }
A30:   return(hDC);
A31:   } /* End of GetPrinterDC(  ) */


/****************************************************************

B01:    FUNCTION: AbortProc()

        PURPOSE:  Processes messages for the Abort Dialog box

****************************************************************/

B02: int FAR PASCAL _export AbortProc(HDC hPr, int Code)
B03:   {MSG msg;

B04:   if(!hAbortDlgWnd)  /* If the abort dialog isn't up yet */
B05:        return(TRUE);

B06:   /* Process messages intended for the abort dialog box */
B07:   while(!bAbort && PeekMessage(&msg, NULL, NULL, NULL,TRUE))
B08:     if(!IsDialogMessage(hAbortDlgWnd, &msg))
```

145

```
B09:        {TranslateMessage(&msg);
B10:        DispatchMessage(&msg);
B11:        }

B12: /*bAbort is TRUE (return is FALSE) if the user has aborted*/
B13:    return (!bAbort);
B14:    } /* End of AbortProc( ) */

****************************************************************

C01:    FUNCTION: AbortDlg(HWND, unsigned, WORD, LONG)

        PURPOSE: Processes messages for printer abort dialog box

        MESSAGES:
            WM_INITDIALOG - initialize dialog box
            WM_COMMAND    - Input received

        COMMENTS
        This dialog box is created while the program is printing,
        and allows the user to cancel the printing process.

****************************************************************/

C02: int FAR PASCAL _export AbortDlg(HWND haDlg, unsigned msg,
     WORD wParam, LONG lParam)
C03:    {switch(msg)
C04:    {/* Watch for Cancel button,RETURN key,ESCAPE key,or
         SPACE BAR */
C05:    case WM_COMMAND:
C06:      return (bAbort = TRUE);

C07:    case WM_INITDIALOG:
C08:      /* Set the focus to the Cancel box of the dialog */
C09:      SetFocus(GetDlgItem(haDlg, IDCANCEL));
C10:      /* Place filename into text */
C11:      SetDlgItemText(haDlg, IDC_FILENAME, szFileName);
C12:      return (TRUE);
C13:    }
C14:    return (FALSE);
C15:    } /* End of AbortDlg( ) */

/****************************************************************/
```

Figure 5-5:   Project PAYUP3

Section 6

Dialog Boxes and the Dialog Editor

The Visual C++ Development System for Windows includes a tool named "AppStudio" (Application Studio) which is accessed from the VWB under menu Tools. This version of AppStudio combines several tools which were originally developed on earlier versions of the C/C++ compiler and the Software Development Kit. Operation of the complete AppStudio is described in the second half of the "User's Guides," a text provided in both the Standard and Professional Programmer's Editions of Visual C++. Within the AppStudio the developer is able to create these types of software products:

- **Menus**—Produced by the Menu Editor. Menu/menu list design is a relatively straightforward task although there are many options open to the designer when the menu has multiple tiers or cascades [Rector 3.1, pp. 624-673]. Menus are one of the subjects of Book 6 in the HOWPS.

- **Accelerator Tables**—Produced by the Accelerator. Table Editor. An accelerator is a two-key combination (e.g., "Ctrl+Z") that initiates the same action as a mouse click, or a series of mouse clicks. If the user must highlight a menu and pick a menu item to perform a task, "Control + Z" tends to be quicker. Hence the name "accelerator." Accelerators are never required in a software application; they only enhance the existing mouse movements [Rector 3.1, pp. 674-678]. See also Book 5 in this series.

- **String Tables**—Produced by the String Table Editor. String tables are included in windows to allow complete change-out of text within an application without disassembling the main project, e.g., converting English language text to Italian language text. String tables are never mandatory in an application [Rector 3.1, pp. 686-689], but they are useful.

- **Graphics**—Produced by the Graphics Editor. These includes icons, cursors, and bitmaps. These are discussed in Book 7 in the HOWPS [See also, Rector 3.1, pp. 329-397, 678-686].
- **Dialogs**—Produced by the Dialog Editor. The remainder of this section deals with dialog boxes and the Dialog Editor [See also, Rector 3.1, pp. 561-621].

Dialog boxes are simple constructs for the developer. If the basic unit of measurement for a dialog box had been selected as the "pixel," where the Standard VGA display is 640 pixels wide by 480 pixels high, then all dimension numbers entered in the dialog box template in the *.RC resource script file would be absolute numbers and would map directly to the video screen presentation. Instead, a variable unit was devised whose size is dependent on the selected font and font size [Rector 3.1, pp. 575-576, and Section 5 of this book, PAYUP1 Popup Dialog Boxes]. In Section 5 the developer was encouraged to change the font in the PAYUP1 dialog boxes from MS Sans Serif to either MS Serif, Times New Roman, Courier, or System to show the changes that occur in a dialog box when the font is changed. A similar exercise will be conducted in this section.

If a developer selects one font to be used for all dialog boxes (e.g., MS Sans Serif), and a standard font size (e.g., 10), then the dialog box creation process becomes simple enough that the Dialog Editor need not necessarily be used to create or edit dialog boxes. The two advantages of the Dialog Editor during dialog box/menu creation over manual creation within the *.RC file are:

- The Dialog Editor displays all static and dynamic entries on the dialog box/menu at one time, allowing the developer to position the elements to obtain an attractive display quickly. If the initial creation is accomplished manually the developer must compile and link the program to view the newly created dialog box/menu each time a change is made, and this is time consuming. However, once the elements are accorded their proper position in the dialog box/menu, manual editing of the *.RC resource script file becomes an easier task than reloading the AppStudio and Dialog Editor to make small changes.
- The Dialog Editor generates additions/corrections to the RESOURCE.H file as the dialogs are created/edited. If the developer manually creates or edits the dialog boxes/menus, care must be taken to modify the RESOURCE.H file manually also.

For these reasons both manual creation and automated Dialog Editor creation processes are discussed in this section.

A typical manually-generated dialog box template is shown below; it is a part of project PAYUP2:

```
CalcBox4  DIALOG  50, 38, 160, 80
STYLE WS_DLGFRAME  |  WS_POPUP
FONT 10, "Ms Sans Serif"
{CTEXT  "Minimum Monthly Payment Is:"     -1, 0,   5, 160, 8
CTEXT   ""                    PUTTEXT1, 15,  40, 12,  SS_CENTER
CTEXT   "Enter Monthly Payment:           -1, 0, 28, 160, 8
EDITTEXT                GETTEXT3, 60, 40, 40, 12,  ES_CENTER
PUSHBUTTON                "OK"    IDOK, 64, 60, 32, 14
}
```

There are three uniquely named elements in this template:

- **Symbolic Name**—CalcBox4. The name is referenced at the time the dialog box is created, in WndProc( ), case WM_COMMAND, wParam = IDM_CALC, case 4. The name is the second argument in statement DialogBox( ), and is enclosed in double quotes because it is an ASCII string. Note that the symbolic name is *not* defined in file PAYUP2.H as an integer.
- **String ID**—PUTTEXT1. This ID, which operates like a handle to the ASCII string, is defined in file PAYUP2.H (#define PUTTEXT1 53).
- **String ID**—GETTEXT3. Same as above, (#define GETTEXT3 54).

With automated creation of dialog boxes in the AppStudio Dialog Editor, each dialog box in a project is given the symbolic name IDD_DIALOGx, where "x" begins at 1 and is incremented for each additional dialog box. However, if a resource script file that was created before the advent of Visual C++ is imported into the AppStudio Dialog Editor, the old symbolic names are used as is (they are not destroyed). Old string IDs are also retained, like GETTEXT1 and PUTTEXT1.

One Important Change: The new dialog box names, like IDD_DIALOG1, are defined as integers in the new automated header file RESOURCE.H. As a result the DialogBox( ) statement's second argument form in WndProc( ) has changed:

> **OLD**—DialogBox(ghWnd,"CalcBox4",haWnd,lpProcDialog1);
>
> **NEW**—DialogBox(ghWnd,MAKEINTRESOURCE(IDD_DIALOG), haWnd,lpProcDialog1);

The automated Dialog Editor system uses names like IDC_EDIT1 and IDC_EDIT2 to assign string IDs (rather than names like PUTTEXT1 and GETTEXT1). The Dialog Editor defines values for these new names in file

RESOURCE.H also. It is necessary that the new file name RESOURCE.H be included at the top of the old header file, *.H, so all templates will execute properly.

The RESOURCE.H file is created when the Dialog Editor is used in a given project to create *or modify* a MENU script or DIALOG script. If the Dialog Editor is never used there will be no RESOURCE.H file in the project (hence it cannot be included at the top of the *.H header file). However, once the Dialog Editor is used to create or modify a MENU or DIALOG, the former *.RC resource script file (which may have been either manually or automatically created) undergoes multiple format changes. However the new *.RC file is compatible with Visual C++ generated projects, old or new.

The remainder of this section deals with two topics:

- Manual dialog box design methods
- Automated dialog box design within the AppStudio Dialog Editor

MANUAL DIALOG BOX DESIGN (MAN-EDIT)

A project named MAN-EDIT has been prepared for a manual design demonstration. The developer is shown two typical dialog boxes and encouraged to try variations in font and font size to determine what is a good standard for future dialog box creations. Once font and font size are affixed there are no surprises in manual dialog box creation.

Load the MAN-EDIT project into the VWB according to the New Project Loading Sequence found at the front of this book. The MAN-EDIT.DEF, .H, .RC, and .C files are listed in Figure 6-1. Once project MAN-EDIT is properly entered into the VWB, choose **Project|Rebuild All MAN-EDIT.EXE** to recompile the project.

Project MAN-EDIT Familiarization   This project will be executed the first time as is, then the developer will be shown the steps to *manually* modify the contents of the dialog boxes. To execute project MAN-EDIT, pick **Project|Execute MAN-EDIT.EXE**. Pick **Begin|Start Manual Edit...**. Two dialog boxes appear on the screen. Both are modeless dialog boxes since two modal dialog boxes cannot appear on the screen at the same time. Both dialog boxes have the same dimensions and same text. They only differ in font: The top dialog box is in font MS Serif and the lower dialog box is in font MS Sans Serif. In the resource script file the upper dialog box is named Dialog1 and the lower is Dialog2.

Do not be concerned that the upper dialog box has a "muted" appearance when compared with the lower dialog box. The upper box does not have the input focus, so it defaults from the thicker frame, style WS_DLGFRAME, to the thinner, less noticeable frame, style WS_BORDER. The lower box has the input focus, and is highlighted on the screen.

Pick the **OK** pushbutton in the lower dialog box to exit the dialog boxes. The MAN-EDIT main window appears; close it by picking the dashbox at the top left corner of the main window (Windows 3.1), or "X" (Windows 95).

To manually edit file MAN-EDIT.RC do the following in the VWB:

1. Pick **File|Open**. The File Open window appears. Under List Files of Type:, pick **All Files [*.*]**.

2. A number of files appear in the FileName: listbox. Pick **man-edit.rc**.

3. File MAN-EDIT.RC appears in its file window. Maximize the window by picking the **up arrow** at the top right of the new window.

4. As a first exercise, in **Dialog1**, change the **MS Serif** font to something else, like **Times New Roman**.

5. Pick **File|Save** to save file MAN-EDIT.RC, then **File|Close** to close the file.

6. Pick **Project|Rebuild All MAN-EDIT.EXE** to recompile the project.

7. When the build is complete, pick **Project|Execute MAN-EDIT.EXE**.

8. In the program, pick **Begin|Start Manual Edit**. Both dialog boxes are displayed, and the upper one is displayed with font Times New Roman (or whatever font was selected).

9. To exit the dialog boxes pick the **OK** pushbutton in the lower dialog box. To exit MAN-EDIT, pick the dashbox or "X."

Try other fonts if you desire, like Arial, etc. Within the AppStudio Dialog Editor these Windows 3.1 English language fonts are available: Arial, Courier, Courier New, Fixedsys, MS Dialog, MS Sans Serif, MS Serif, Small Fonts, System, and Times New Roman. Windows 95 adds several additional fonts. Find a font that you like, then set both dialog boxes to this font in the *.RC file for the next step.

Now experiment with font size. For example, set the top box to font size 8 and the lower box to font size 10 (these are the most common dialog box fonts). Pick the one you like best. Remember that users who wear glasses (especially those with bifocals) prefer font size 10 or even larger, whereas the younger set

151

accepts font 8. If few words are included in the dialog box the font size may be increased to 12.

Why are you doing this? Because once you have selected an appropriate dialog box font and font size, dialog box sizes become uniform from application to application. For example, if the font selected is MS Sans Serif and the font size is 10, then the full screen is about 275 units wide and 215 units high when the display is set to Standard VGA. The developer may perform most simple dialog box work from the basic template shown in project MAN-EDIT, Figure 6-1, lines 219-235, because approximate dimensions are known for the dialog box and its contents.

Book 1   Figure 6-1

```
Program MAN-EDIT files:
  1.  *.DEF, module-definition file
  2.  *.H,   header file
  3.  *.RC,  resource script file
  4.  *.C,   WinMain( ), WndProc( ), AboutProc( ), DialogProc( )


/***************************************************************/

001: ; MAN-EDIT.DEF module-definition file -- used by LINK.EXE
002: NAME  ManualEditDlgBox ;  Application's module name
003: DESCRIPTION  'Manually Edit a Dialog Box'
004: EXETYPE WINDOWS     ;  Required for all Windows applications
005: STUB  'WINSTUB.EXE'; Generates error message if application
                         ;  is run without Windows
006: ;CODE can be moved in memory and discarded/reloaded
007: CODE  PRELOAD MOVEABLE DISCARDABLE
008: ;DATA must be MULTIPLE if program invoked more than once
009: DATA  PRELOAD MOVEABLE MULTIPLE
010: HEAPSIZE    1024


/***************************************************************/

101: /* MAN-EDIT.H (header file) */
102: #define IDM_ABOUT   10
103: #define IDM_DIALOG  20


/***************************************************************/

201: /* MAN-EDIT.RC (resource script file) */
202: #include <windows.h>
203: #include "man-edit.h"
```

```
204: Man-EditMenu MENU
205:    {POPUP        "&Begin"
206:       {MENUITEM "&About Man-Edit...", IDM_ABOUT
207:       MENUITEM "&Start Manual Edit...", IDM_DIALOG
208:       }
209:    }


210: AboutBox DIALOG 22, 12, 110, 55
211: STYLE DS_MODALFRAME | WS_CAPTION
212: CAPTION "About Man-Edit Window"
213: FONT 10, "MS Sans Serif"
214:    {CTEXT "Manual Edit Application"    -1, 0,  5, 110,  8
215:    CTEXT "Microsoft Windows 3.1 and 4.0" -1, 0, 15, 110,  8
216:    CTEXT "Copyright \251 R. Braden, 1994" -1, 0, 25, 110,  8
217:    PUSHBUTTON "OK"                    IDOK, 39, 36,  32, 14
218:    }


219: Dialog1  DIALOG 62, 5, 160, 80
220: STYLE WS_DLGFRAME | WS_POPUP | WS_VISIBLE
221: FONT 10, "Ms Serif"
222:    {CTEXT "G O   T I G E R S   !"        -1, 0, 15, 160,  8
223:    CTEXT "Beat Perfunctory Institute of Technology"
                                             -1, 0, 25, 160,  8
224:    CTEXT "I am 160 units wide and 80 units high"
                                             -1  0, 35, 160,  8
225:    CTEXT "My top-left corner is at coordinates 62, 5"
                                             -1, 0, 45 160,  8
226:    }


227: Dialog2  DIALOG 62,105, 160, 80
228: STYLE WS_DLGFRAME | WS_POPUP | WS_VISIBLE
229: FONT 10, "Ms Sans Serif"
230:    {CTEXT "G O   T I G E R S   !"        -1, 0, 15, 160,  8
231:    CTEXT "Beat Perfunctory Institute of Technology"
                                             -1, 0, 25, 160,  8
232:    CTEXT "I am 160 units wide and 80 units high"
                                             -1, 0, 35, 160,  8
233:    CTEXT "My top-left corner is at coordinates 62, 105"
                                             -1, 0, 45, 160,  8

234:    PUSHBUTTON "OK"                    IDOK, 64, 60,  32, 14
235:    }

/****************************************************************/

301: /* MAN-EDIT.C , R. Braden */
```

```
302: #define STRICT
303: #include <windows.h>
304: #include <stdlib.h>
305: #include "man-edit.h"

306: long FAR PASCAL _export WndProc(HWND, UINT, WPARAM, LPARAM);
307: BOOL FAR PASCAL _export AboutProc(HWND, UINT,WPARAM,LPARAM);
308: BOOL FAR PASCAL _export DialogProc(HWND,UINT,WPARAM,LPARAM);

309: HANDLE hInst;
310: HWND   ghWnd; /* Global handle for main window */
311: HWND ghDlgM1, ghDlgM2; /* Modeless dialog boxes */

312: BOOL CloseBoxes;

313: int PASCAL
     WinMain(HINSTANCE hInstance,HINSTANCE hPrevInstance,
     LPSTR lpCmdLine, int nCmdShow)
314:  {MSG msg;
315:  WNDCLASS wc;
316:  ATOM aWndClass; /* Test for proper window registration */

317:  hInst = hInstance;

318:  /* Register main window */
319:  if(!hPrevInstance)
320:    {wc.style = NULL;
321:    wc.lpfnWndProc = WndProc;
322:    wc.cbClsExtra = 0;
323:    wc.cbWndExtra = 0;
324:    wc.hInstance = hInst;
325:    wc.hIcon = LoadIcon(NULL, IDI_APPLICATION);
326:    wc.hCursor = LoadCursor(NULL, IDC_ARROW);
327:    wc.hbrBackground = GetStockObject(WHITE_BRUSH);
328:    wc.lpszMenuName = "Man-EditMenu";
329:    wc.lpszClassName = "Man-EditWClass";
330:    aWndClass = RegisterClass(&wc);
331:    if(!aWndClass)
332:      MessageBox(NULL,
           "Failure to Register Main Window Class.",NULL,MB_OK);
333:    }

334:  /* Create the main window */
335:  ghWnd = CreateWindow("Man-EditWClass",
         "Manual Edit of Dialog Boxes",
         WS_OVERLAPPEDWINDOW | WS_MAXIMIZEBOX  |  WS_MINIMIZEBOX,
         CW_USEDEFAULT,CW_USEDEFAULT,CW_USEDEFAULT,CW_USEDEFAULT,
```

```
                NULL, NULL, hInst, NULL);

336:    /* Make main window visible; update its client area */
337:    /* ShowWindow(ghWnd, nCmdShow); */
337A:   ShowWindow(ghWnd, SW_SHOWMAXIMIZED);
338:    UpdateWindow(ghWnd);

339:    /* Main message queue */
340:    while(GetMessage(&msg, NULL, NULL, NULL))
341:       {TranslateMessage(&msg);
342:       DispatchMessage(&msg);
343:       }

344:    return (msg.wParam);
345:    } /* End of WinMain( )  */


/****************************************************************/

401: long FAR PASCAL _export
     WndProc(HWND haWnd,UINT msg,WPARAM wParam,LPARAM lParam)
402:    {DLGPROC lpProcAbout;  /* Pointer to  "AboutProc( )" */
403:    DLGPROC lpProcDialog1;  /* Ptrs to "DialogProc( )" */
404:    DLGPROC lpProcDialog2;
405:    switch(msg)
406:       {case WM_COMMAND:
407:          if(wParam == IDM_ABOUT) /* Modal dialog box */
408:             {lpProcAbout=(DLGPROC)MakeProcInstance((FARPROC)
                   AboutProc, hInst);
409:             DialogBox(hInst, "AboutBox", haWnd, @PROGRAM = lpProcAbout);
410:             FreeProcInstance((FARPROC)lpProcAbout);
411:             }

412:          else if(wParam == IDM_DIALOG)
413:             {CloseBoxes = FALSE;
414:             /* Modeless dialog box, "Dialog1" */
415:             lpProcDialog1=(DLGPROC)MakeProcInstance((FARPROC)
                   DialogProc, hInst);
416:             ghDlgM1 = CreateDialog(hInst,"Dialog1",haWnd,
                   lpProcDialog1);

417:             /* Modeless dialog box, "Dialog2" */
418:             lpProcDialog2=(DLGPROC)MakeProcInstance((FARPROC)
                   DialogProc, hInst);
419:             ghDlgM2 = CreateDialog(hInst,"Dialog2",haWnd,
                   lpProcDialog2);
420:             }
```

155

```
421:       return 0;

422:    case WM_DESTROY:
423:      if(CloseBoxes)
424:        {FreeProcInstance((FARPROC)lpProcDialog1);
425:        FreeProcInstance((FARPROC)lpProcDialog2);
426:        CloseBoxes = FALSE;
427:        }
428:      else
429:        PostQuitMessage(0);

430:      break;

431:    default:
432:       return(DefWindowProc(haWnd, msg, wParam, lParam));
433:      }
434:    return NULL;
435:    } /* End of WndProc( ) */


/*****************************************************************/

501: BOOL FAR PASCAL _export
     DialogProc(HWND haDlg,UINT msg,WPARAM wParam,LPARAM lParam)
502:    {switch(msg)
503:      {case WM_INITDIALOG:
504:        return TRUE;

505:      case WM_COMMAND:
506:        if(wParam == IDOK)
507:          {CloseBoxes = TRUE;
508:          PostMessage(ghDlgM2, WM_CLOSE, 0, OL);
509:          return TRUE;
510:          }

511:       break;

512:      case WM_CLOSE: /* Close modeless dialog boxes */
513:        DestroyWindow(ghDlgM1);
514:        DestroyWindow(ghDlgM2);
515:        PostMessage(ghWnd, WM_DESTROY, 0, OL);
516:        return TRUE;

517:      } /* End of switch(msg) */
518:    return FALSE;
519:    } /* End of DialogProc( ) */


/*****************************************************************/
```

```
601: BOOL FAR PASCAL _export
     AboutProc(HWND haAbout,UINT msg,WPARAM wParam,LPARAM lParam)
602:  {switch(msg)
603:    {case WM_INITDIALOG:
604:      return TRUE; /* Set focus to pushbutton */

605:    case WM_COMMAND:
606:      if(wParam == IDOK || wParam == IDCANCEL)
607:        {EndDialog(haAbout, TRUE);
608:        return TRUE;
609:        }
610:      break;
611:    }
612:  return FALSE;
613:  } /* End of AboutProc( ) */


/*************************************************************/
```

Figure 6-1: Listing of project MAN-EDIT

AUTOMATED DIALOG BOX DESIGN WITH APPSTUDIO DIALOG EDITOR (AUTOEDIT and NEWEDIT)

This is the alternative method of creating dialog boxes. Two demonstrations are included:

- **Project AUTOEDIT**—Importing an existing *.RC file into the Dialog Editor and editing an *existing* dialog box. The new *.RC file which emerges after edit is different in format but compatible with the Visual C++ system even though its *.RC file looks quite different from the original *.RC file.

- **Project NEWEDIT**—Importing an existing *.RC file into the Dialog Editor and adding a new dialog box template to it. The resulting *.RC file includes a mix of old and new, but still works in Visual C++ so long as the newly created RESOURCE.H file is included in the old *.H header file and the MAKEINTRESOURCE( ) macro is used as the second argument in the DialogBox( ) statement that begins creation of the new dialog box.

The writer has not addressed the last alternative for Dialog Editor usage: using an empty *.RC file created by AppWizard for a totally new project. This Dialog Editor usage will be included in a later book.

AUTOEDIT—Editing a Preexisting Dialog Template   The same files that were loaded into project MAN-EDIT are also located in project AUTOEDIT.

Load the AUTOEDIT project into the VWB according to the New Project Loading Sequence found at the front of this book.

This project includes an extra file, AUTOEDIT.RCA, which is a second copy of file AUTOEDIT.RC. During this exercise file AUTOEDIT.RC will be changed from the manual format to the automated format by the Dialog Editor. To redo the exercise later, copy file AUTOEDIT.RCA to AUTOEDIT.RC and continue. The change in AUTOEDIT.RC format occurs the first time the file is saved in the Dialog Editor.

Once AUTOEDIT is loaded into the VWB, pick **Tools|AppStudio**. Under Type: (Dialog or Menu) pick **Dialog**. Three dialogs appear in the Resources: listbox: ABOUTBOX, DIALOG1, and DIALOG2. Double-click on **DIALOG1**.

When the "DIALOG1" (Dialog) window appears the dialog box will be located at the top-left of the screen and its top-left corner cannot be relocated. This does *not* represent its display location in the working project; its true screen coordinates are shown at the bottom-right of the screen on the status bar. To change a dialog box's true screen coordinates, pick either **Window|Show Properties** or **Resource|Properties**. When the Dialog Properties window appears, the X Pos: and Y Pos: numbers are editable by clicking on the appropriate editbox. To exit the Dialog Properties window, pick the dashbox at the top left of the window.

TIP: Within a *complete* dialog box's Dialog Properties window there are two windows: General Properties and Style Properties. The developer toggles between these two windows by picking either General or Style at the top-right corner of the window. For the present time the default settings in the Style window of this dialog box are acceptable. When any subelement in the dialog box is selected and that subelement's Dialog Properties window is opened, it will only have General Properties—no Style Properties. Style pertains to the total dialog box, not its subelements.

To change the size of a dialog box in the Dialog Editor main window, use the mouse to pick and drag one side of the box on the Dialog Editor screen (or pick and drag a corner to shrink or enlarge both width and height dimensions at the same time). As this is being accomplished, the width and height numbers in the status bar at the bottom of the screen change continuously. Recall that all dialog box sizing numbers are dependent on the font selected and the font size. If these selections change, the sizing numbers change.

TIP: Once you have selected a font and font size for the dialog box, you may determine the allowable maximum "width" for that dialog box by dragging the right edge of the box to the right edge of the screen. The width number shown in the status bar at the lower-right of the screen is the maximum. If, for example, you pick a MS Sans Serif font with font size 10, the maximum width number is approximately 275. This number may be used later if dialog box horizontal centering is desired. For example, if a dialog box width of 200 is used, then the top left corner X coordinate of the box for centering is (275 - 200) / 2, or 37.

Two tool bars are displayed. The top tool bar belongs to the AppStudio and includes icons for file operations (on the left) and special icons (on the right). The contents of this tool bar are explained in the AppStudio Version 1.0 User Manual, Table 1.1, page 5. The fourth icon from the left, the "undo" icon, allows the developer to move backward in the design as many as 10 steps to undo mistakes.

The lower tool bar belongs exclusively to the Dialog Editor. Its icons are defined in the AppStudio Version 1.0 User Manual, Figure 3.10, page 51.

At this point in the demonstration the developer has loaded project AUTOEDIT into the VWB, picked the AppStudio tool, picked Type: **Dialog**, and picked Resource: DIALOG1. The Window|Show Properties window was shown to explain where the dialog box top left screen coordinate is edited. Then it was shown how the dialog box size may be changed by dragging its lower-right corner with the mouse. Note that some element in the Dialog Editor is *always* highlighted (has the focus). If a subelement in the dialog box is picked with the mouse, then it has the focus. But as soon as the developer clicks on any open part of the Dialog Editor window, the entire dialog box receives the focus.

The present task of this demonstration is to change the font in DIALOG1 from FONT 10, MS Serif to FONT 10, Times New Roman, the same change that was suggested in project MAN-EDIT.

1. Pick **Window|Show Properties** again. Because the dialog box is highlighted, the Dialog Properties window appears. The General Properties should be displayed (not the Style Properties). If Style Properties are shown, toggle the switch at the upper right of the window

159

to return to General Properties. Pick the **Font** pushbutton at the lower-left of the window.

2. The Font window appears. Pick **Times New Roman** from the list of fonts. Notice that a font size of 12 is not available with Times New Roman. Pick **OK** to exit the Font window.

3. Pick the dashbox at the top left of the Dialog Properties window to exit (this is the dashbox created by the WM_SYSMENU window style), or the window may be quasi-exited by picking on the main Dialog Editor window interior. However, picking the main Dialog Editor window does not "close" the Dialog Properties window, it simply moves it behind the larger window. This is no big deal unless a developer chooses the Dialog Properties window 100 times in succession—now a large collection of "thunks" of unused code is building in the program execution region. All the windows which are not properly closed during Dialog Editor execution are destroyed (fortunately) when the Dialog Editor is exited.

   Why didn't the manufacturer place an "Exit" or "OK" pushbutton in the windows that support the Dialog Editor? They probably took up too much room in the window. Note that these support windows tend to be as small as possible.

4. The main Dialog Editor window is now displayed. To save the dialog box, pick **File|Save**.

TIP: Do not pick the "test" switch, which is the leftmost icon on the Dialog Editor tool bar, because this dialog box has no active element in it (no pushbutton, radio button, etc.). If the developer picks the test icon, the Dialog Editor system hangs.

5. A warning window appears, stating that you are about to overwrite a resource script file which was *not* created in AppStudio. Overwrite? Pick **YES**.

6. To exit the Dialog Editor, pick **File|Close**.

7. To exit AppStudio, pick **File|Exit**.

The main Visual Workbench (VWB) window appears. To examine the new *.RC file, do the following:

8. Pick **File|Open**. The Open File window appears.

9. Under List Files of Type: pick **All Files[*.*]**.

9. In the file name list box pick **autoedit.rc**.

The new *.RC file is now displayed. If a hardcopy of the file is desired, pick **File|Print** on the VWB window.

To recompile the project, pick **Project|Rebuild All AUTOEDIT.EXE**. To execute the project, pick **Project|Execute AUTOEDIT.EXE**. The two dialog boxes will appear on the main window just as they did earlier, but the upper dialog box displays a Times New Roman font, point size 10.

This demonstration shows that the new *.RC file generated by the Dialog Editor is compatible with the older project files in AUTOEDIT.

NEWEDIT—Creating a New Dialog Template in an Old *RC File
NEWEDIT is a new project, and includes one dialog box.

Load the NEWEDIT project into the VWB according to the New Project Loading Sequence found at the front of this book.

This project includes an extra file, NEWEDIT.RCA, which is a second copy of file NEWEDIT.RC. During this exercise file NEWEDIT.RC will be changed from the manual format to the automated format by the Dialog Editor. To re-do the exercise later, copy file NEWEDIT.RCA to NEWEDIT.RC and continue. The change in NEWEDIT.RC format occurs the first time the file is saved in the Dialog Editor.

The NEWEDIT.RC file is unusual in that it includes only the template for the AboutBox. The template for a dialog box, which will be named "IDD_DIALOG1," is to be created by the developer in the Dialog Editor. The "hooks" for IDD_DIALOG1 are already in file NEWEDIT.C, procedure WndProc( ), message WM_COMMAND, wParam = IDM_DIALOG. These are shown in Figure 6-2, page 166, lines 413-415, which must be enabled after the dialog box is created. In file NEWEDIT.H one line (line 102 in Figure 6-2) must also be enabled to include the new header file RESOURCE.H in the project.

After loading NEWEDIT into the VWB:

1. Pick **Tools|AppStudio**. The AppStudio - NEWEDIT.RC [Resource Script] window appears.

2. In window Type: pick **Dialog**.

3. In Resources: listbox, ABOUTBOX appears. However, a new dialog box is to be created, so pick **New...** at the lower left of the main window.

4. The New Resource window appears. Pick **Dialog**, then pick **OK**.

5. A prototype dialog box appears with two pushbuttons (OK and Cancel). The status bar at the bottom of the screen shows that the top-left coordinate of the dialog box is 0,0 and the size is 185 x 92.

6. Pick **Window|Show Properties** or **Resource|Properties**. The Dialog Properties window appears.

7. Pick the **Font** pushbutton (lower left) and set font to Arial (or some other font). Pick a font size. Pick **OK** to exit the Font window.

8. In the Dialog Properties window set X Pos: = 58 and Y Pos: = 40. Note that dialog box has been assigned a symbolic name of IDD_DIALOG1. Pick the dashbox at the top left to exit the Dialog Properties window.

9. Move both pushbuttons about 1 inch to the left (click and drag) so the dialog box may be decreased in size. Then drag the lower-right corner of the dialog box up and to the left until the size shown in the status bar is 160 x 80.

10. Pick the **Cancel** pushbutton (highlight it). Pick **Edit|Delete** and the pushbutton disappears.

11. Drag the **OK** pushbutton to the center, lower part of the dialog box.

12. From the Toolbox, click on the big **A** and drag it into the dialog box. Release the mouse button. The word "Static" appears in the box. Drag the left and right sides of the highlighted box out to the limits of the dialog box.

13. Pick **Resource|Properties** while the Static box is still highlighted. A Dialog: Text Properties window appears. Set Text Align: to **Center**. In the Caption: editbox where the word Static appears, replace Static with **Go Turtledoves !**. Pick the dashbox at the top left of the Dialog: Text Properties window to exit.

14. Pick **A** three more times and place three more static texts into the dialog box:

```
"----------------------------------"
"Knock 'em down, roll 'em around,"
"A little bit of dirt won't hurt."
```

15. Position the elements until the dialog box looks something like that shown on Figure 6-3, page 168. Note that any highlighted element may be moved up, down, left, or right using the keyboard arrow keys.

The next step involves saving what has been created. Highlight the entire dialog box.

16. Pick **File|Save**. A warning window appears, stating that a new NEWEDIT.RC file will be created. Pick **Yes**. At this point a new header file, RESOURCE.H is generated by the Dialog Editor.

17. Pick **File|Close** to exit the Dialog Editor.

18. Pick **File|Exit** to exit AppStudio.

19. Enter file NEWEDIT.C and enable lines 413-415 (Figure 6-2).

20. Enter file NEWEDIT.H and enable line 102 (Figure 6-2).

In the VWB pick **Project|Rebuild All**—NEWEDIT.EXE. Or pick the **Project|Rebuild All** icon, which is the seventh icon from the right, on the VWB tool bar. This icon has three arrows pointing down onto a group of papers. To execute project NEWEDIT, pick **Project|Execute NEWEDIT .EXE** or pick the **Run** icon, which is the fourth icon from the right on the VWB tool bar.

QUESTION: What happens if the developer forgets to include file RESOURCE.H at the top of file NEWEDIT.H ?

ANSWER: The dialog box is skipped by the program, which does not know that it exists.

If you prefer a dialog box without a caption (title bar) and System menu dashbox, re-enter the Dialog Editor, reselect the dialog box, open the Dialog Properties window, select **Style** at the upper right part of the box, and deselect the caption and sysmenu checkboxes.

This completes the discussion of dialog boxes and the Dialog Editor.

Book 1   Figure 6-2

```
Program NEWEDIT files:
  1.  *.DEF, module-definition file
  2.  *.H,   header file
  3.  *.RC,  resource script file
  4.  *.C,   WinMain( ), WndProc( ), AboutProc( ), DialogProc( )

/*************************************************************/

001: ; NEWEDIT.DEF module-definition file -- used by LINK.EXE
002: NAME  CreateNewDlgBox  ;  Application's module name
003: DESCRIPTION  'Create a new dialog box using Dialog Editor'
004: EXETYPE WINDOWS     ;  Required for all Windows applications
005: STUB  'WINSTUB.EXE'; Generates error message if application
```

```
                           ;  is run without Windows
006: ;CODE can be moved in memory and discarded/reloaded
007: CODE   PRELOAD MOVEABLE DISCARDABLE
008: ;DATA must be MULTIPLE if program invoked more than once
009: DATA  PRELOAD MOVEABLE MULTIPLE
010: HEAPSIZE      1024
```

/**/

```
101: /* NEWEDIT.H (header file) */
102: /* #include "resource.h" */
103: #define IDM_ABOUT   10
104: #define IDM_DIALOG  20
```

/**/

```
201: /* NEWEDIT.RC (resource script file) */
202: #include <windows.h>
203: #include "newedit.h"
204: NewEditMenu MENU
205:   {POPUP        "&Begin"
206:     {MENUITEM "&About NewEdit...", IDM_ABOUT
207:     MENUITEM "&Start New Edit...", IDM_DIALOG
208:     }
209:   }
210: AboutBox DIALOG 22, 12, 110, 55
211: STYLE DS_MODALFRAME | WS_CAPTION
212: CAPTION "About NewEdit Window"
213: FONT 10, "MS Sans Serif"
214:   {CTEXT "Manual Edit Application"     -1,  0,  5, 110,  8
215:    CTEXT "Microsoft Windows 3.1 and 4.0" -1,  0, 15, 110,  8
216:    CTEXT "Copyright \251 _____, 1994" -1,  0, 25, 110,  8
217:    PUSHBUTTON "OK"                    IDOK, 39, 36,  32, 14
218:   }
```

/**/

```
301: /*  NEWEDIT.C, R. Braden */

302: /******************************************************************/
     /* THE DEVELOPER MUST CREATE ONE DIALOG BOX IN NEWEDIT.RC */
     /* TO SUPPORT THIS PROJECT. THE DIALOG EDITOR ASSIGNS THE */
     /* NAME "IDD_DIALOG1" TO  THIS DIALOG  BOX  AND CREATES A */
     /* SECOND HEADER  FILE NAMED "RESOURCE.H" DURING THE SAVE */
     /* PROCESS  THAT DEFINES  THE  NEWLY  CREATED  SYMBOLICS. */
     /* THIS NEW FILE  RESOURCE.H  MUST BE INCLUDED IN THE OLD */
     /* HEADER FILE, NEWEDIT.H.                                */
```

```
      /*                                                   */
      /* NOTE THAT IN THE  DialogBox( , , , ) STATEMENT  BELOW, */
      /* THE SECOND ARGUMENT  IS "MAKEINTRESOURCE(IDD_DIALOG1)" */
      /* RATHER THAN THE OLDER ENTRY, "IDD_DIALOG1".            */
      /********************************************************/

303: #define STRICT
304: #include <windows.h>
305: #include <stdlib.h>
306: #include "newedit.h"
307: long FAR PASCAL _export WndProc(HWND, UINT, WPARAM, LPARAM);
308: BOOL FAR PASCAL _export AboutProc(HWND, UINT,WPARAM,LPARAM);
309: BOOL FAR PASCAL _export DialogProc(HWND,UINT,WPARAM,LPARAM);
310: HANDLE hInst;
311: HWND   ghWnd; /* Global handle for main window */

312: int PASCAL
     WinMain(HINSTANCE hInstance,HINSTANCE hPrevInstance,
       LPSTR lpCmdLine, int nCmdShow)
313: {MSG msg;
314: WNDCLASS wc;
315: ATOM aWndClass; /* Test for proper window registration */

316: hInst = hInstance;

317: /* Register main window */
318: if(!hPrevInstance)
319:   {wc.style = NULL;
320:   wc.lpfnWndProc = WndProc;
321:   wc.cbClsExtra = 0;
322:   wc.cbWndExtra = 0;
323:   wc.hInstance = hInst;
324:   wc.hIcon = LoadIcon(NULL, IDI_APPLICATION);
325:   wc.hCursor = LoadCursor(NULL, IDC_ARROW);
326:   wc.hbrBackground = GetStockObject(WHITE_BRUSH);
327:   wc.lpszMenuName = "NewEditMenu";
328:   wc.lpszClassName = "NewEditWClass";
329:   aWndClass = RegisterClass(&wc);
330:   if(!aWndClass)
331:     MessageBox(NULL,
          "Failure to Register Main Window Class",NULL,MB_OK);
332:   }

333: /* Create the main window */
334: ghWnd = CreateWindow("NewEditWClass",
       "Practice Using Dialog Editor",
       WS_OVERLAPPEDWINDOW | WS_MAXIMIZEBOX  | WS_MINIMIZEBOX,
```

```
           CW_USEDEFAULT,CW_USEDEFAULT,CW_USEDEFAULT,CW_USEDEFAULT,
           NULL, NULL, hInst, NULL);

335:   /* Make main window visible; update its client area */
336:   /* ShowWindow(ghWnd, nCmdShow); */
337:   ShowWindow(ghWnd, SW_SHOWMAXIMIZED);
338:   UpdateWindow(ghWnd);

339:   /* Main message queue */
340:   while(GetMessage(&msg, NULL, NULL, NULL))
341:     {TranslateMessage(&msg);
342:     DispatchMessage(&msg);
343:     }
344:   return (msg.wParam);
345:   } /* End of WinMain( )  */

/***************************************************************/

401: long FAR PASCAL _export
     WndProc(HWND haWnd, UINT msg, WPARAM wParam, LPARAM lParam)
402:   {DLGPROC lpProcAbout;   /* Pointer to  "AboutProc( )" */
403:   DLGPROC lpProcDialog1;   /* Pointer to "DialogProc( )" */

404:   switch(msg)
405:     {case WM_COMMAND:
406:       if(wParam == IDM_ABOUT) /* Modal dialog box */
407:         {lpProcAbout=(DLGPROC)MakeProcInstance((FARPROC)
            AboutProc, hInst);
408:         DialogBox(hInst, "AboutBox", haWnd, lpProcAbout);
409:         FreeProcInstance((FARPROC)lpProcAbout);
410:         }
411:       else if(wParam == IDM_DIALOG)
412:         {/* Create modal dialog box, "IDD_DIALOG1" */
413:       /* lpProcDialog1=(DLGPROC)MakeProcInstance((FARPROC)
            DialogProc, hInst);
414:         DialogBox(hInst,MAKEINTRESOURCE(IDD_DIALOG1),haWnd,
            lpProcDialog1);
415:         FreeProcInstance((FARPROC)lpProcDialog1);
416:       */ }
417:       return 0;

418:     case WM_DESTROY:
419:       PostQuitMessage(0);
420:       break;
421:     default:
422:       return(DefWindowProc(haWnd, msg, wParam, lParam));
         }
```

```
423:    return NULL;
424:    } /* End of WndProc( ) */

/***************************************************************/

501: BOOL FAR PASCAL _export
     DialogProc(HWND haDlg,UINT msg,WPARAM wParam,LPARAM lParam)
502:    {switch(msg)
503:      {case WM_INITDIALOG:
504:        return TRUE;
505:      case WM_COMMAND:
           /* OK pushbutton in dialog box sends control here */
506:        if(wParam == IDOK)
507:          {PostMessage(ghWnd, WM_DESTROY, 0, 0L);
508:          return TRUE;
509:          }
510:        break;
511:      } /* End of switch(msg) */
512:    return FALSE;
513:    } /* End of DialogProc( ) */

/***************************************************************/

601: BOOL FAR PASCAL _export
     AboutProc(HWND haAbout,UINT msg,WPARAM wParam,LPARAM lParam)
602:    {switch(msg)
603:      {case WM_INITDIALOG:
604:        return TRUE; /* Set focus to pushbutton */
605:      case WM_COMMAND:
606:        if(wParam == IDOK || wParam == IDCANCEL)
607:          {EndDialog(haAbout, TRUE);
608:          return TRUE;
609:          }
610:        break;
611:      }
612:    return FALSE;
613:    } /* End of AboutProc( ) */

/***************************************************************/
```

Figure 6-2:   Listing of NEWEDIT

Figure 6-3:   Dialog Box

Section 7

Debugging With the Visual C++ Integrated Debugger

This section briefly demonstrates selected capabilities of the Visual C++ Integrated Debugger. Chapter 11 in the *Visual Workbench User's Guide* describes how to perform the principal tasks to prepare for and conduct debugging sessions.

"Debugging" provides the capability to move at normal CPU speed through a series of machine instructions, then pause at one selected instruction to display values for the variables involved in the execution at that stage of the program. The point at which this "pause" occurs is called a breakpoint.

This book outlines these debugging tasks:

- Setting and removing breakpoints.
- Using the watch window, which is capable of displaying values for several global variables and/or several local variables at each breakpoint in the program.
- Using quick watch, which displays the value of one selected global or local variable at a time.

Previous editions of MS debuggers set up special source code listings that were operated upon by the developer to set breakpoints and display values for selected variables. The Visual C++ integrated debugger accomplishes all tasks within the original source code (*.C) listing. Values for the selected variables are displayed in special popup windows. Color is used extensively in the display to reveal locations of breakpoints, etc.

The project to be used to demonstrate a debugging capability in Visual C++ is named DEBUG. Project DEBUG copies one file from a source location to a target location; the source/target keyboard entries must be made by the developer during execution of this program in the debugger. The source code includes a copy of function CopyOneFile( ), which is an integral part of project SETUP1. SETUP1 transfers HOWPS Book 1 source code from an installation diskette to the developer's hard disk. SETUP1 is also included on the Book 1 installation diskette for information, and is transferred to directory SETUP1 on your hard disk during setup.

DEBUGGING ICONS ON THE VWB TOOLBAR VWB Toolbar is described in the Version 1.0 VWB User's Guide, pp. 60-63. The six icons on the right side of the toolbar are used in debugging. This demonstration will use three of the six icons:

- **Breakpoint**—Sixth icon from the right (open hand), used to set/reset a breakpoint.
- **QuickWatch View**—Fifth icon from the right (a pair of spectacles), used to view a selected variable's value(s) while execution is suspended at a breakpoint.
- **Run**—Program run icon, fourth from the right.

The StepIn, StepOver, and StepOut icons are enhancements on the basic debugging process.

If the developer is interested in "Hard" versus "Soft" mode debugging, read pages 196-198 in the Version 1.0 VWB User's Guide.

TWO DEBUGGING METHODS Visual C++ offers two slightly different procedures for observing the values of local/global variables at each breakpoint in the program. These are:

- **QuickWatch Method** This method allows the developer to highlight the name of one variable in the source code while program execution is suspended at a selected breakpoint and display the value of that variable. As soon as that variable's value is displayed the developer is free to choose another variable, display its value, etc. The principal limitation with this method is that only one variable is displayed at a time.
- **Stodgy Method** This method provides for the developer who wants to observe the values of many variables at a given breakpoint, and does not want to sequence through the variable list with the Quick Method. To accomplish this task it is necessary for the debugger to create a temporary file in which the values of the list of variables could be written. This is the "Watch" file.

All procedures are the same for both methods until the first breakpoint is reached in the debugging session.

Demonstration Preparation   For test purposes, place a formatted diskette in drive A or B and create a directory named BOOK1 on the diskette. Copy a file, e.g., AUTOEXEC.BAT, to the BOOK1 directory on the diskette as a file named "TESTFILE.XXX." Next, move to hard disk drive C and create a directory named GOGO at the root.

Demonstration   To begin, load DEBUG into the VWB according to the New Project Loading Sequence found at the front of the book.

Build project DEBUG by picking **Project|Rebuild All DEBUG.EXE**, then execute the build by picking **Project|Execute DEBUG.EXE**. There are two inputs to the program:

- The first user entry is the name of the file to be copied, with complete path, e.g., B:\BOOK1\TESTFILE.XXX.
- The second user entry is the new location and new name for the file. This program does not recognize copy-codes such as "*.*", etc. Try C:\GOGO\TESTFILE.XXX.

As soon as the file has been copied a completion message is posted on the screen. This sequence confirms that the project executes properly.

The debugger will be used to suspend the action at two points in the program, to examine the form and content of the file names and their complete paths.

Figure 7-1, page 175, is a copy of the source code in DEBUG; the line numbers along the left edge match the line numbers assigned in the VWB file listings. When this section refers to "line 168 in CopyProc( )" for example, that line number will appear on the Figure 7-1 listing *and* will be line 168 on the VWB screen.

PREPARING A FILE FOR DEBUGGING (BREAKPOINT INSERTION)   All breakpoint insertions or removals are made on the *.C source code file as it appears in the VWB. This is possible because the Build Mode in the Project Options window was set to Debug originally (and will remain in the Debug mode until it is ready for commercial release).

Project DEBUG is loaded into the VWB. Pick **File|Open** and pick file DEBUG.C for editing. Pick the **Maximize** up-arrow at the top-right of the screen to get full-screen editing.

SETTING BREAKPOINTS Two breakpoints will set in the DEBUG.C file.

1. Move to line 168. Highlight this line by clicking on its left edge with the left mouse button, holding the button down, and dragging the mouse to the right (past the text). Release the mouse button.

2. Pick the **Toggle Breakpoint** icon (sixth from the right, open hand).

3. Line 168 in file DEBUG.C is now highlighted in red. (To deselect this breakpoint, highlight line 168 again and pick the Toggle Breakpoint icon again.)

4. Move to line 192. Highlight this line.

5. Pick the **Toggle Breakpoint** icon.

6. Line 192 is now highlighted in red.

EXECUTE DEBUG.EXE Pick the **Run** icon (fourth from the right).

1. Dialog Box #1 appears.

2. Type a suitable dummy input file name, such as **B:\TMPBOOK1\ TESTFILE.XXX.**

3. Pick **OK** to exit the window.

File DEBUG.C is displayed and line 168, the first breakpoint, is highlighted in yellow (to show that the program is suspended at this breakpoint).

QuickWatch Method Demonstration This method allows the developer to observe the value of one variable at a time.

1. Move to line 156 and highlight variable **pathstring1**.

2. Pick the **QuickWatch View** icon (the spectacles).

3. The QuickWatch window appears and displays the contents of the ASCII string pathstring1. To exit the Quick Watch window, pick **Close**.

4. Move to line 180 and highlight variable **pathstring2**.

5. Pick the **QuickWatch View** icon (spectacles).

6. The QuickWatch window appears, and displays the contents of the ASCII string pathstring2 (which is empty for now). Pick pushbutton **Close** to exit.

7. Pick the **Run** icon on the VWB toolbar (fourth from the right). Dialog box #2 appears.

8. Type a suitable dummy output file name, such as **C:\GOGO\ TESTFILE.XXX**.

9. Pick **OK** to exit the window.

   File DEBUG.C is displayed and line 192, the second breakpoint, is highlighted in yellow (to show that the program is suspended at this breakpoint).

10. Move to line 156 and highlight variable **pathstring1**.

11. Pick the **QuickWatch View** icon (the spectacles).

12. The QuickWatch window appears and displays the contents of the ASCII string pathstring1 (which has not changed since it was displayed earlier). To exit the window, pick **Close**.

13. Move to line 180 and highlight variable **pathstring2**.

14. Pick the **QuickWatch View** icon (spectacles).

15. The QuickWatch window appears and displays the contents of the ASCII string pathstring2 (which contains the output file path and name). Pick **Close** to exit.

16. Pick the **Run** icon on the VWB toolbar (fourth from the right) to complete execution of the program.

This ends the QuickWatch Method demonstration.

Stodgy Method Demonstration This method allows the developer to observe the value of several variables at a time by creating a temporary file to contain the list of variables. Recall that breakpoints have already been set at lines 168 and 192.

1. Re-execute DEBUG.EXE. Pick the **Run** icon (fourth from the right). Dialog box #1 appears.

2. Type a suitable dummy input file name, such as **B:\TMPBOOK1\ TESTFILE.XXX**.

3. Pick **OK** to exit the window.

   File DEBUG.C is displayed and line 168, the first breakpoint, is highlighted in yellow (to show that the program is suspended at this breakpoint).

4. Pick **Window|Watch** from the VWB toolbar.

5. A window Microsoft Visual C++ - DEBUG.MAK <2> Watch appears, and the cursor is blinking at the first empty line in the file.

6. Type **pathstring1** and press the <Enter> key.

   A "+" sign appears in front of pathstring1 to show that this variable can be expanded (it is an ASCII string). Expand it by double-clicking on the name pathstring1. This produces a long ASCII character list similar to that shown in the QuickWatch method.

7. Scroll down to the first empty line in the file, type **pathstring2**, and press <Enter>. The "+" sign appears in front of pathstring2 also. Expand it by double-clicking on the name pathstring2.

   At this point the values of all chars in both ASCII strings pathstring1 and pathstring2 are displayed at the same time.

8. Exit the window by picking **File|Close**. Pick the **Run** icon on the VWB toolbar (fourth from the right). Dialog Box #2 appears.

9. Type a suitable dummy output file name, such as **C:\GOGO\ TESTFILE.XXX**.

10. Pick **OK** to exit the window.

    File DEBUG.C is displayed and line 192, the second breakpoint, is highlighted in yellow (to show that the program is suspended at this breakpoint).

11. Pick **Window|Watch** to display the values of both pathstring1 and pathstring2. The temporary file created earlier to display multiple variables reappears. Close the temporary file.

12. Pick the **Run** icon on the VWB toolbar (fourth from the right), to complete execution of the program.

End of Stodgy Method demonstration.

TIP: To clear ALL breakpoints in any *.C file:

1. Pick **Debug|Breakpoints** on the VWB toolbar.
2. The Breakpoints window appears. Pick pushbutton **Clear All** at the lower right of the window.
3. Pick **Close** to exit the Breakpoints window.

This clears all breakpoints in the file. The writer normally picks **File|Save As** and **OK** to ensure that all unnecessary debugging information is removed from the file for next time.

This ends the discussion of the Visual C++ Integrated Debugger.

Book 1   Figure 7-1

This is a special listing of the executable code in project DEBUG. The line
numbers along the left edge match the line numbers in the VWB file listing.
Line #

```
 1  /*  DEBUG.C, R. Braden */

 3  #define STRICT

 5  #define BUFFER_SIZE 4096L  /* Define buffer size */

 7  #include <windows.h>
 8  #include <stdio.h>
 9  #include <io.h>  /* For _lseek( ) in CopyOneFile( ) */
10  #include <stdlib.h>
11  #include <string.h>

13  #include "debug.h"

15  long FAR PASCAL _export WndProc(HWND, UINT, WPARAM, LPARAM);
16  BOOL FAR PASCAL _export CopyProc(HWND, UINT, WPARAM,LPARAM);
17  int  FAR PASCAL _export CopyOneFile(LPSTR, LPSTR);

19  HANDLE hInst;
20  HWND   ghWnd;
21  int    nCOUNTER;

23  char pathstring1[40], pathstring2[40];
24  char szTemp[80];

26  int PASCAL
    WinMain(HINSTANCE hInstance,HINSTANCE hPrevInstance,
      LPSTR lpCmdLine, int nCmdShow)
29    {MSG msg;
30    WNDCLASS  wc;

32    if(!hPrevInstance)
33      {/* Main window */
34      wc.style = NULL;
35      wc.lpfnWndProc = WndProc;
36      wc.cbClsExtra = 0;
37      wc.cbWndExtra = 0;
38      wc.hInstance = hInstance;
39      wc.hIcon = LoadIcon(NULL, IDI_APPLICATION);
40      wc.hCursor = LoadCursor(NULL, IDC_ARROW);
```

```
41    wc.hbrBackground = GetStockObject(WHITE_BRUSH);
42    wc.lpszMenuName = NULL;
43    wc.lpszClassName = "DebugWClass";
44    RegisterClass(&wc);
45    }

47    hInst = hInstance;

49    /* Create a main window for this application instance. */
50    hWnd = CreateWindow("DebugWClass",
         "Demonstrate Debug Application",
         WS_OVERLAPPEDWINDOW,1,60,630,400,NULL,NULL,hInst,NULL);
53    ShowWindow(ghWnd, nCmdShow);
54    UpdateWindow(ghWnd);

56    nCOUNTER = 1 ; /* Start the program sequence */
57    PostMessage(ghWnd, WM_COMMAND, IDM_COPY, OL);

59    while(GetMessage(&msg, NULL, NULL, NULL))
60      {TranslateMessage(&msg);
61      DispatchMessage(&msg);
62      }
63    return(msg.wParam); /* Returns value from PostQuitMsg */
64    } /* End of WinMain( ) */

/***************************************************************/

68  long FAR PASCAL _export
    WndProc(HWND haWnd,UINT msg,WPARAM wParam,LPARAM lParam)
70    {DLGPROC lpPS;   /* Pointer to "CopyProc" function */

72    switch(msg)
73      {case WM_COMMAND:
74        if(wParam == IDM_COPY)
75          {switch(nCOUNTER)
76            {case 1:
77               lpPS=(DLGPROC)MakeProcInstance((FARPROC)
                   CopyProc,hInst);
79             DialogBox(hInst, "Box1", haWnd, lpPS);
80             FreeProcInstance((FARPROC)lpPS);
81             break;
82            case 2:
83             lpPS=(DLGPROC)MakeProcInstance((FARPROC)
                   CopyProc,hInst);
85             DialogBox(hInst, "Box2", haWnd, lpPS);
86             FreeProcInstance((FARPROC)lpPS);
87             break;
```

```
88        case 3:
89          lpPS=(DLGPROC)MakeProcInstance((FARPROC)
              CopyProc,hInst);
91         DialogBox(hInst, "Box3", haWnd, lpPS);
92         FreeProcInstance((FARPROC)lpPS);
93          break;
94        case 4:
95          lpPS=(DLGPROC)MakeProcInstance((FARPROC)
              CopyProc,hInst);
97         DialogBox(hInst, "Box4", haWnd, lpPS);
98         FreeProcInstance((FARPROC)lpPS);
99          break;
100      }
101    break;
102    }

104    else
105    return(DefWindowProc(haWnd, msg, wParam, lParam));

107    case WM_DESTROY:
108      PostQuitMessage(0);
109      break;

111    default:
112      return(DefWindowProc(haWnd, msg, wParam, lParam));

114   return (NULL);
115   } /* End of WndProc( ) */

/****************************************************************/

119 BOOL FAR PASCAL _export
    CopyProc(HWND haDlg,UINT msg,WPARAM wParam,LPARAM lParam)
121 {int nS1, nS2, JJ, success;
122 HWND lhDummy;

124   switch(msg)
125     {case WM_INITDIALOG:
126       switch(nCOUNTER)
127         {case 1: /* Set input focus to edit box, GETTEXT1 */
128            lhDummy = (HWND)GetDlgItem(haDlg, GETTEXT1);
129            SetFocus(lhDummy);
130            return FALSE;
131         case 2:  /* Set input focus to edit box, GETTEXT2 */
132            lhDummy = (HWND)GetDlgItem(haDlg, GETTEXT2);
133            SetFocus(lhDummy);
134            return FALSE;
```

```
135        case 3:  /* Place GETTEXT1 in box */
136          SetDlgItemText(haDlg, PUTTEXT1,
                 (LPSTR)&pathstring1[0]);
138          SetDlgItemText(haDlg, PUTTEXT2,
                 (LPSTR)&pathstring2[0]);
140          /* Set input focus to YES pushbutton */
141          return TRUE;
142        case 4: /* Set input focus to OK pushbutton */
143          return TRUE;
144        } /* End of switch(nCOUNTER) */
145      break;

147    case WM_COMMAND:
148      switch(nCOUNTER)
149        {case 1:  /* File to be copied */
150         if(wParam == IDOK || wParam == IDCANCEL)
151           {nS1 = GetDlgItemText(haDlg,GETTEXT1,
                 (LPSTR)&pathstring1[0],40);

154          /* Check for blanks in the path */
155          for(JJ = 0; JJ < nS1; JJ++)
156            if(pathstring1[JJ] == ' ')
157              {MessageBox(ghWnd,
                    "No blank spaces allowed in path.",
                    NULL, MB_OK);
160              EndDialog(haDlg, TRUE);
161              nCOUNTER = 1; /* Start all over again */
162              PostMessage(ghWnd, WM_COMMAND, IDM_COPY,OL);
163              return TRUE;
164              }

166          EndDialog(haDlg, TRUE);
167          nCOUNTER = 2; /* Set up the next popup window */
168          PostMessage(ghWnd, WM_COMMAND, IDM_COPY, OL);
169          return TRUE;
170          }
171        break;

173      case 2:  /* New file to be created */
174         if(wParam == IDOK || wParam == IDCANCEL)
175           {nS2 = GetDlgItemText(haDlg,GETTEXT2,
                 (LPSTR)&pathstring2[0],40);

178          /* Check for blanks in the path */
179          for(JJ = 0; JJ < nS2; JJ++)
180            if(pathstring2[JJ] == ' ')
181              {MessageBox(ghWnd,
```

```
                   "No blank spaces allowed in path.",NULL,
                   MB_OK);
184                EndDialog(haDlg, TRUE);
185                COUNTER = 1; /* Start all over again */
186                PostMessage(ghWnd, WM_COMMAND, IDM_COPY,OL);
187                return TRUE;
188                }

190                EndDialog(haDlg, TRUE);
191                nCOUNTER = 3; /* Set up the next popup window */
192                PostMessage(ghWnd, WM_COMMAND, IDM_COPY, OL);
193                return TRUE;
194                }
195             break;

197           case 3: /*  Entry is _____  */
198             if(wParam == IDNO)
199                {nCOUNTER = 1; /* Re-cycle for corrected data */
200                EndDialog(haDlg, TRUE);
201                PostMessage(ghWnd, WM_COMMAND, IDM_COPY, OL);
202                return TRUE;
203                }
204             else if(wParam == IDYES)
205                {nCOUNTER = 4;
206                EndDialog(haDlg, TRUE);

208                success = CopyOneFile(pathstring1, pathstring2);

210                if(success != 0)
211                   {MessageBox(ghWnd,
                         "Failure to copy file.",NULL,MB_OK);
213                   PostMessage(ghWnd, WM_DESTROY, 0, OL);
214                   return TRUE;
215                   }

217                PostMessage(ghWnd, WM_COMMAND, IDM_COPY, OL);
218                return TRUE;
219                }

221          case 4:
222             if(wParam == IDOK || wParam == IDCANCEL)
223                {PostMessage(ghWnd, WM_DESTROY, 0, OL);
224                return TRUE;
225                }
226             break;
227          } /* End of switch(nCOUNTER) */
228       break;
```

```
229      } /* End of switch(msg) */
230    return FALSE;
231    } /* End of CopyProc( ) */

/*************************************************************/

235  int FAR PASCAL _export CopyOneFile(LPSTR S1, LPSTR S2)
236  {/* To keep stack overflow  from occurring,  this function
        tranfers "BUFFER_SIZE" number  of bytes at a time from the
        original file to the new file */
239  HFILE OldWinFH, NewWinFH;
240  FILE  *OldFH, *NewFH;
241  OFSTRUCT OfStruct1, OfStruct2;
242  long pos;
243  int jj, bytesread, byteswritten, intquot, intrem;
244  char buffer[BUFFER_SIZE + 20];
245  ldiv_t ldiv_result;

247    /* Open original file */
248    if((OldWinFH = OpenFile((LPSTR)S1, (LPOFSTRUCT)&OfStruct1,
            OF_READ)) == NULL)
250      {MessageBox(ghWnd, "Unable to open original file.",
          NULL, MB_OK);
252      return -1;
253      }
254    else /* Convert window file handle to DOS file pointer */
255      {if((OldFH = fdopen(OldWinFH, "r")) == NULL)
256        {MessageBox(ghWnd,
              "Cannot locate original file.",NULL,MB_OK);
258        return -1;
259        }
260      }

262    /* Determine length of the original file */
263    pos = _lseek(OldWinFH, 0L, SEEK_END);
264    if(pos == -1L)
265      {MessageBox(ghWnd,
            "Unable to locate end of original file.",NULL, MB_OK);
267      return -1;
268      }
269    else
270      {sprintf(szTemp, "Length of old file = %ld .",pos);
271      MessageBox(ghWnd, szTemp, NULL, MB_OK);
272      ldiv_result = ldiv(pos,BUFFER_SIZE);
273      /*Answers are in ldiv_result.quot and ldiv_result.rem */
274      }
```

```
276    /* Open new file to copy old file into */
277    if((NewWinFH = OpenFile((LPSTR)S2, (LPOFSTRUCT)&OfStruct2,
           OF_CREATE)) == NULL)
279    {MessageBox(ghWnd,
         "Unable to open new file for copying.", NULL, MB_OK);
281    return -1;
282    }
283    else /* Convert new window file handle to DOS file ptr */
284    {if((NewFH = fdopen(NewWinFH, "w")) == NULL)
285      {MessageBox(ghWnd,
        "Unable to convert output win handle to DOS file ptr.",
           NULL, MB_OK);
288    return -1;
289      }
290    }

292    /* Transfer chars from old to new */
293    intquot = (int)ldiv_result.quot;
294    rewind(OldFH); /* Move file pointer back to origin */

296    for(jj = 0; jj < intquot; jj++)
297      {if((bytesread = fread(buffer,(int)BUFFER_SIZE,1,OldFH))
         <= 0)
299      {MessageBox(ghWnd,
           "Cannot read data from old file.", NULL, MB_OK);
301    return -1;
302      }

304      if((byteswritten = fwrite(buffer,(int)BUFFER_SIZE,1,
         NewFH))==-1)
306      {MessageBox(ghWnd,
           "No data written to new file.", NULL, MB_OK);
308    return -1;
309      }
310    }

312    /* Transfer the last segment of the file */
313    intrem = (int)ldiv_result.rem;
314    if((bytesread = fread(buffer, intrem, 1, OldFH)) <= 0)
315      {MessageBox(ghWnd,
           "Old file read failure on last segment.", NULL,MB_OK);
317    return -1;
318      }

320    if((byteswritten = fwrite(buffer, intrem, 1,NewFH)) <= -1)
321      {MessageBox(ghWnd,
           "New file write failure on last segment.",NULL,MB_OK);
```

```
323      return -1;
324      }

326   /* Close files */
327   fclose(OldFH);
328   fclose(NewFH);
329   return 0; /* Signal successful completion of task */
330   } /* End of CopyOneFile( ) */

/****************************************************************/
```

Figure 7-1:   Listing of project DEBUG

Section 8

Strict Typecasting

This section demonstrates one advantage of STRICT typecasting, the ability to locate arguments within procedure calls that are illegally typecast. The project STRICT will be used for the demonstration.

Load the STRICT project into the VWB according to the New Project Loading Sequence found at the front of this book. Rebuild All, and execute the program. There are several modes in which the program will "hang," so all of them cannot be described here. The developer may recycle the program several times by doing the following within STRICT:

1. Pick **Begin|Start Strict**.

2. Capture the lower-right corner of the main window with the mouse and drag it to a new location.

3. Pick **Begin|Start Strict** again.

   The program will eventually hang. But why? It compiled and linked successfully!

After the PC is turned off and restarted, the VWB is reloaded, and project STRICT is reloaded into the VWB, the hanging question can be answered.

1. In the VWB pick **File|Edit** and pick file **STRICT.C**.

2. Enable the first statement in the file #define STRICT by removing the comment marks.

3. Save file STRICT.C, and recompile using **Project|Rebuild All STRICT.EXE**.

   This time compilation will not succeed. STRICT typecasting will detect two errors where the handle **hdc** is incorrectly entered in place of the correct handle **haWnd** [in the EndPaint( ) statements].

4. Replace the two incorrect hdc entries with haWnd, recompile the program, and execute it.

The program should recycle forever.

How important is STRICT typecasting? You be the judge.

TIP: The developer will soon discover that there is a class of functions within the C/C++ language whose arguments are "overloaded," which means that they assume different typecastings based on the particular use of the function. STRICT cannot comprehend this, and will issue warnings no matter what the developer does. When this occurs, the writer compiles using the "#define STRICT" definition once to clear up any mis-typecastings, then disables STRICT for the ensuing work so the overload warnings will not appear.

The three most common overloaded executable statements are:

- **CreateWindow( ), argument #9** This argument is typecast as a HMENU, yet is used by every child window as a type UINT. To eliminate a recurring warning message by the compiler, the child window identifier is recast to type HMENU (for example):

   ```
   (HMENU)IDC_SCROLL1
   ```

- **SendMessage( ) or PostMessage( ), argument #3** This argument is typecast as a WPARAM, but is often used to send a handle name of type HWND to another function. To eliminate the recurring warning message by the compiler, the argument #3 parameter is recast to type WPARAM:

   ```
   (WPARAM)lhPointer
   ```

Section 9

SETUP Example

The setup program for this book is included in directory SETUP1 in case the developer has questions on how one transfers files from a diskette to a hard disk automatically.

The setup task would be greatly simplified if the user were never asked to enter a directory in the path. Commercial software manufacturers recognize this fact and offer a "standard" installation with each application that loads the software into directories on the user's hard disk which are preselected by the manufacturer. For example, the Visual C++ Development System for Windows offers a standard installation that copies all necessary code to a directory named MSVC.

SETUP1 offers the developer the choice of directories where the Book 1 software is to be loaded, so it is somewhat complicated in its procedures.

Section 10

Book 1 Closure

As the developer has progressed through the MAINMAIN, PAYUP, EDIT, DEBUG, and STRICT projects, he/she should have a better understanding of these techniques:

- General sequence of windowed program events
- Main window constructs
- Program startup techniques
- Modal popup dialog box and message box constructs
- File generation and printing within a Windows program
- How to use the Dialog Editor, or construct manual dialog box templates
- How to use the integrated debugger
- The advantages of STRICT typecasting

In addition, the developer has gained an initial familiarity with the Visual Workbench (VWB). The developer will find the on-line references helpful, and entry into the helps becomes easier as one learns the windows jargon and the operation of the search schemes within the help files. The new nomenclature is difficult to learn.

If the developer compares the non-windowed PAYUP code of Figure 5-2 with the windowed code of Figure 5-5, the first thing he notices is that the windowed source code is four or five times larger than the non-windowed code! It's a little like comparing the number of parts under the hood of your modern automobile to the number of parts under a 1948 automobile hood. The piece-parts-list has certainly grown, but so has the performance of the vehicle.

The performance of programs written in MS Windows is awesome indeed. The developer has, at her/his fingertips, hundreds of prewritten macros that perform most common computer tasks in a consistent manner. We can now move up to the higher-order languages with ease once we iron out the kinks in the present windows development systems.

Are there kinks in the present windows system? You bet. What are you, the developer, going to do in the meantime, until all the kinks are ironed out? You will probably do as developers have always done—keep a copy of every piece of working windows code you write (to use as examples in the future) and hope that you can overcome the peculiarities of the current, resident windows compiler faster than the manufacturer inserts new peculiarities into the new compilers.

Book 1 SETUP Diskette Files List

These files should be located on the Book 1 SETUP diskette:

- SETUP1.EXE (in root directory)
- Ten projects with extensions: C, OBJ, EXE, DEF, H, RC, MAK, RES, VCW (nine extensions in all):
  - NEW-PROJ (plus five more files below)
  - MAINMAIN
  - PAYUP2
  - PAYUP3
  - MAN-EDIT
  - AUTOEDIT
  - NEWEDIT
  - DEBUG
  - STRICT
  - SETUP1
- One project (PAYUPNW) with three extensions: C, OBJ, EXE.
- One project (PAYUP1) with eight extensions: C, OBJ, EXE, DEF, H, RC, MAK, RES.
- One project (WINDLIST) with three extensions: DOC, VCW, MAK.
- Five files added to the NEW-PROJ directory:
  - GENERATE.DEF
  - GENERATE.H
  - GENERATE.RC
  - GENERATE.C
  - GENERATE.MAK

- Extra files MAN-EDIT.RCA, AUTOEDIT.RCA, and NEWEDIT.RCA, which are second copies of files MAN-EDIT.RC, AUTOEDIT.RC, and NEWEDIT.RC.

The file SETUP1.EXE transfers 112 files to the hard disk.

Total number of files on the diskette is 113.

Index

_export, 74

A

AbortDlg( ), 124
AbortProc( ), 124, 126
About Box, 49
About Box Construct, 65
AboutBox( ), 80
AboutProc( ), 65, 67
Accelerator Tables, 147
AppStudio, 27
AppWizard, 33, 49
ATOM, 74
AUTOEDIT, 157
AUTOEXEC.BAT, 21

B

BeginPaint( ), 76
BOOL, 52, 57
Build Mode 31
BuildMode, 27

C

CalcProc( ), 80
CALLBACK, 57
CAPTION, 66
child window controls, 45
Child Windows, 41, 46
CHILDTEM, 58
CODE, 51
COMMDLG.LIB, 130
Courier, 98
CreateDC( ), 145
CreateDialog( ), 40

CreateFont( ), 141
CreatePen( ), 76
CreateWindow( ), 39, 44, 63, 75, 90, 96, 100
CreateWindowEx( ), 68, 96
Creating Administrative Projects, 35
Creating Successive Projects, 34
CS_VREDRAW | CS_HREDRAW, 53, 58, 74
CTEXT, 66, 89, 97
CW_USEDEFAULT, 63

D

DATA, 51
Debugging, 169
DefWindowProc( ), 58, 76
DeleteDC( ), 142, 144
DeleteObject( ), 143
DESCRIPTION, 51
desktop, 61
DestroyWindow( ), 143, 156
DIALOG, 66, 97
Dialog Editor, 148
DialogBox( ), 40, 68, 76, 91, 100, 103
Dialogs, 148
Disabling the Browser Database, 25
Disabling VWB Tabs, 24
DispatchMessage( ), 75, 91
DLGPROC, 91
double, 113
DS_MODALFRAME, 56, 66